Great Chapters

A Year with God in His Story

Table of Contents

Acknowledgments

This book would not have been possible without the contribution of Janet Henjum whose love for the Lord motivated her, even during a difficult illness, to tirelessly use her gifts of detail and language in completing the labor of editing the contents.

Thank you also to Melanie Haubrich who used her artistic gifts to communicate God's love in the design of the cover and then worked diligently to ensure the final product was of the highest standard.

Thank you to my children, their spouses, and our friends who used this book as a devotional and gave helpful feedback to improve the message of God's love and grace.

Most of all, thank you to my wife, Marie, who prayed for this project and helped edit and sort through content. Her attention to detail and support is impossible to put into words.

Introduction

There have been many Bible reading plans to help one get through the precious Word of God. The ultimate goal is that God would get through to us. The weekly format of reading a great chapter, devotion, and study plan included in these pages is designed with this ultimate goal in mind.

Sometimes when reading the Bible, we are in a sort of conundrum. If we focus our reading and studying on selected verses, we can be left without an awareness of the context of a passage. As a result, the richness of God can be missed or misconstrued. On the other hand, if we are reading the Bible from beginning to end, Genesis to Revelation, we have the necessary context to understand God's story, but for various reasons we can get caught in the details or lost in a list of names or laws. We can miss the message.

Selecting important chapters and studying them is the method of this book. Reading these chapters can help us to stay focused on the main truths of the Scriptures. This is not to discourage selecting verses or reading the Bible from cover to cover. The chapter reading approach in this book is chosen to encourage context and enhance the depth of God's message to us.

These great chapters are organized in two ways. First, there is a chronological order. The chapters begin in the Old Testament with Genesis and end in the New Testament with Revelation. Second, there is a seasonal order. During the season of Easter, the chapters shift to the New Testament for the resurrection account. During Christmas, the birth accounts of Jesus are considered. At the end of the 52 great chapters, there are seven extra devotions, chapters, and studies for the special times of the year when our hearts are focused on God's purpose for the Bible summarized in John 3:16.

The devotion offered each week summarizes or highlights a portion of the accompanying great chapter. The devotions have three foci: to provide comfort from God as we face adversity in life, to grow us as Christians, and to direct us to Jesus and the Gospel. He alone brings peace and hope. He is the only force that truly transforms us for the good. He loves us. He saves us. He empowers us to live a life of meaning and purpose. Jesus speaks often in the Bible about the fact that He is the Vine and we are the branches. Apart from Him, we can do nothing (John 15:5). When our lives are, by the power of the Holy Spirit, experiencing the fullness of His love and grace, we think, decide, and act like Him.

The prayers offered at the end of each devotion are useful as they are written. They may also serve as a prayer-starter. There may be an idea or thought that may help us to meditate on God and His Word. Prayer is communication with the living God. It was always meant to be more than something quickly spoken or read.

Likewise, the questions, thoughts to ponder, and Bible verses at the end of each devotion are meant as a beginning to study God's Word. They are a possible direction for learning and growing in the grace and knowledge of our Lord and Savior Jesus Christ (2 Peter 3:18). The weekly structure of the great chapters allows for time to journal, meditate, and dig deeper into a topic, historical context, or parallel passage. The great chapters' structure encourages personal study and application.

There are other great chapters that could have been selected. Some personal favorites may not be included in this list. All of the Bible is God's Word and life-giving. For each of us, it reveals Jesus, our lifelong Companion and Friend. May we be drawn into all of God's Word and walk with Him day by day.

Week 1: A Year in the Word?

Read Psalm 1 – Blessed is the Person

"Sometimes we just don't know what to do..." Frustrated and discouraged, Paul Newman spoke those words to a jury struggling with a difficult case in the movie, *The Verdict*. In one way or another, we have all experienced moments of indecision. "What do I do..." ...in this relationship? ...with my educational future? ...in the midst of this moral decision? ...in this issue of discipline? ...with my retirement plan? The journey of life is not always easy or clear.

Even as Christians, we struggle with what to do. We wonder, "How much do I give?" "What do I say to my neighbor who is not Christian?" "How do I get my daughter or son to be connected to Christ and His Church?" "What do I pray?" There are not always black and white answers to these questions. Sometimes, there is blessing simply in the asking of these questions, simply in the struggle to search for answers, but that doesn't always satisfy us at the time of asking.

Despite all of this uncertainty and questioning, there are only two paths during our time on this earth. God is crystal clear about this in the Bible. We are either with God or without God—righteous or wicked. Yes, black and white is not so comfortable for us. Our culture loves gray with multiple options and everybody's-truth-is-relevant. Sure, this sounds very closed-minded—even over-simplified—but this is what God says in the Bible: Two ways.

A life with God is lived in Christ with a Biblical view ("...*delighting in the law of the Lord, and on it meditating day and night.*"). A life with God is fresh, dynamic, and renewing ("...*planted by streams of water.*"). When we are with God, we apply the appropriate fruit (love, joy, peace, patience, kindness, goodness, gentleness, faithfulness, self-control) at the right time, in the right way, with the right motivation ("...*which yields its fruit in season*"), and experience the blessing of the right outcome ("...*whatever he does prospers*").

God is the creator of all that is good. When everything went awry because of sin, God, in Jesus Christ, saved us. The Holy Spirit blesses us with faith every day. Living with God means experiencing: God's creation in all of its goodness, forgiveness when we fail, and victory over death forever.

To live without God is death. Since God is life and purpose and hope and love, to go through 70 or 80 or 90 years without Him would mean never truly comprehending life—never joining in the dance for which He designed us. God calls those who head down that path wicked. They merely take up space on the planet ("...*they are like chaff that the wind blows away.*") because they never join God in His plan to bring healing to a world that is desperately struggling for hope and love. Spending the here and now without God is a choice to spend forever without God ("...*the wicked will not stand in the judgment nor sinners in the assembly of the righteous.*"), which is called hell.

There are only two ways to live: with God or without God; life or death; righteous or wicked. The Bible is difficult to understand in some ways, but not about this. Sin and Satan have made the world cloudy and grey, but this distinction is absolute, definite, and certain. The truth about the reality life with and without God is crystal clear.

But what's even more amazingly and wonderfully clear is that God loves us. He wants us with Him. He calls us. He initiates and invites us into relationship and life. He plants us by living waters—the Bible and people to study and pray with us. He blesses us with prosperity here on earth and hereafter in heaven. He makes living with Him possible. During this next year, will you let Him walk with you? Will you stand in Him? Will you sit at His feet?

Lord God, it sounds so clear when You put it the way that You do in Psalm 1. Help me to see with the clarity that You give the truth about living with You. Give me obedience and discipline this year so that I can be consistent in worship, study, prayer, and devotions. Let me be planted by streams of water, yield fruit in season, like a leaf not wither, so that all that I do will prosper for You and Your Kingdom. In Jesus' powerful name I pray. Amen.

Questions to consider:

1. Read 1 John 1:5-7. Note the difference (darkness and light) you will notice when walking without God and walking with God. Walking is daily. How are you walking these days?

2. What will keep you from walking with the Lord this year? What might you do to overcome these obstacles? What can you do to follow through in the study of God's Word this year?

3. What one thing can you do to stay more in step with the Lord this year?

4. What can you (your family) do to stay faithful to the Lord?

Week 2: The Way It Is Supposed to Be

Read Genesis 1 – Creation

Death is not the way it is supposed to be.
Broken relationships...not the way it is supposed to be.
War and crime...not the way it is supposed to be.
Pain...not the way it is supposed to be.

At some level, we all understand this. In fact, Genesis 1 makes it clear that when God created this universe, His intent was life, community, joy, goodness, health...and it would last forever.

A quick glance at God in Genesis 1 reveals:
- The Trinity was present—Father, Son (The Word), and Holy Spirit. All the members of the Trinity were totally engaged in creating the heavens and the earth.
- God spoke the universe into existence, creating something out of nothing.
- Everything created was good.
- Human beings were the crown of creation.

A quick glance at human beings at the time of creation reminds us:
- God intended us for relationship with Him.
- God made us to join Him in managing His creation for the good.
- God created us to be in relationship with other people and His world.

Our culture tries to convince us that suffering is inevitable. Religions like Buddhism suggest we should just accept the way that it is. And many people do. We give in and give up. We think that God does not care and certainly won't get involved in our problems. We adopt a philosophy of living that forgets the uniqueness and wonder of human beings, replacing it with disregard for the sanctity of human life and acting with the values of animals. We push God away—not conversing with Him or even considering Him—as if He simply did not exist. We see ourselves as the source of living, making our lives all about me instead of being good stewards of the environment and resources He (the true Source) gave us. We live as if other people and their gifts are to be consumed rather than loved.

The creation account returns us to the magnificence of God, His love for us, and our purpose for living. We are grounded again in the truths about God and us. He is the Creator of light and life. From Him all goodness comes.

We are the created. When we see that this world is not as it was supposed to be, we are moved immediately to God for the solution. We are directed to the cross where the sacrifice of Jesus Christ paid the price for the destructiveness of sin. We are saved through that sacrifice—not just to exist but to make a positive difference. We are lifted from the drab, meaningless monotony to flourish in relationship with God, blessing the lives of others and our amazing world.

Father, Son, and Spirit, how easy it is to lose sight of You. I confuse the Creator and creation, elevating myself to a position that leaves me empty. As I contemplate this universe, remind me again of Your awesome power and my value in You. Direct me to the salvation that You have won for me so that I can be a servant to others and a witness of Your love. In Jesus' name. Amen.

Questions to consider:

1. What does the creation account teach you to think when you are out in nature? What does the creation account teach you about taking care of the environment?

2. Make a list of the repeated phrases in Genesis 1 (such as "And God said..."). What does each of these phrases teach you about the Creation?

3. Based on Genesis 1, how would you describe our intended relationship with God? With other people? What impact does that have on your friendships, marriage, and/or family?

4. Read John 1 and compare it to Genesis 1. How does John help you to understand Genesis?

Week 3: What Went Wrong? Who Set It Right?

Read Genesis 3 – The Fall into Sin

A recent Internet blog[1] stated that there is no such thing as cold. Cold is simply a word to describe the lack of heat. The blog continued by asserting that there is no such thing as darkness. Darkness is simply a word to describe the lack of light. The reasoning followed that there is no such thing as evil; it is just a word to describe the absence of God or God's way of doing things. What do you think about that thought? What does Genesis 3 say about these ideas?

The Bible begins with a creation that is perfectly good. It is all proceeding the way that God wants it. He is walking with humans in the garden in perfect relationship, perfect partnership. God has done the amazing work of creating and then invited humankind into managing the creation with Him...for good. There is perfect peace or *shalom*. The world is as it should be—the way God wants it.

Meanwhile, we on earth don't see what has been going on in heaven. We don't see that one of God's angels has decided to rebel against God and His ways or that a number of angels join the rebellion against God. They want control. They don't think that they need God or His ways of good. They will be like God and establish their own ways. Since God is God, these traitors are kicked out of heaven and thrown to the earth. There they continue to define what we call evil. They are antagonistic and vindictive wanting to infect all of the goodness of God...which brings us to the serpent and Eve and temptation.

The original temptation of humankind had all of the unimaginative repetition of our temptations—the same old challenge to God's truth and consequences; the same old lies about God not being the source of goodness; the same old empty, superficial promises of satisfaction if I do my thing rather than God's. And, of course, Adam and Eve fell for the deception, the quick fix, the easy way. They chose to move away from God's plan and, with it, His love and goodness, even

---

[1] Numerous blogs speak to the question, "Does cold really exist?"

8

blaming God (Genesis 3:12). They joined the rebel turned devil and all of his demons in defining evil. Would we do any differently?

The best part of this account is the solution. The good news of the Gospel shows up as soon as God shows up. In verse 15, God offers the first promise of a Savior: "...he (Jesus) shall bruise your (Satan's) head, and you shall bruise his heel (Jesus' death on the cross)." There would be many more prophecies to come.

In their sin, Adam and Eve recognized their nakedness and vulnerability. They attempted to cover themselves with fig leaves. God covers (the Hebrew word for *cover* is the same root word meaning *forgive*) and clothes them (v. 21) with animal skins. This covering would be more effective and permanent. Imagine their horror at seeing the shedding of blood for the first time. But death would lead to life. Thus begins a crimson thread of blood that runs through the Bible always pointing to the ultimate shedding of blood on Calvary.

God sets things right again. He calls Adam and Eve out of their hiding. He invites them back into His plan. He loves them. Yes, there were consequences to this rebellion, this sin, and they were dire. Blaming and fear and guilt and death are ugly and painful. But the promise was mind-boggling.

God's own Son would pay the consequences. Jesus would face the blame and the fear and the guilt and the death. In one final cosmic battle on the cross, He would fix things. He would again invite humankind, not into partnering with Satan to define evil but into partnership with God to put peace and goodness—*shalom*—back in creation. Humankind would be saved from the fallout of the fall. We can have relationship with God again. We can live with Him here but, even more, in a return to the garden—in heaven. Perfection restored. No more evil because God is permanently and perfectly present.

Lord Jesus, when all was lost, You found me. You brought me into relationship at Baptism. My sin was forgiven. Death was defeated. As I consider again the fall from You and Your plan, I am overwhelmed that You continued to call, continued to love, and continued to care. I am amazed that You consider me a worthy partner with You in restoring peace and goodness to this creation. Thank You and help me never to lose sight of this gift of life that You give. In Your name I pray. Amen.

Questions to consider:

1. Do you want to seek God and His good? Do you live in the light? Do you walk with the Creator and Savior of the world? In what ways might you be hiding from Him or keeping Him from restoring this good relationship?

2. What are you doing to join God in His original plan to bring about *shalom* to the creation? What evil are you helping to set right by bringing Jesus Christ into the situation or relationship or community?

3. When sin came into the world, Adam and Eve had some new experiences (hiding from God, etc.). Make a list of the differences in the world that became their reality. How do those same devastating experiences show themselves in your life? Think through the ripple effect of sin.

4. Notice that God covered the nakedness (vulnerability?) of Adam and Eve with something permanent, something that required an innocent death and the shedding of blood. What does this tell you about God and what He has done for you?

Week 4: How to Fix the World

Read Genesis 6 – The Flood

Have you ever wanted God to "take out" someone who is mean and uncaring, who hurts you and is oblivious to it? James and John, two of Jesus' disciples did (Luke 9:52-55). I would guess that many of us have as well. Sometimes we just want justice and are convinced that our brand of justice is the best. Our thinking is, "If this hurtful, self-focused person were not in my life, my life would be so much better. And besides, that person is just taking up space on the planet, so no great loss."

In Genesis 6, God sees the corruption of people who live to be hundreds of years old. They are full of pride and selfishness. They have taken the great creation of God and the life that He has given them and made it "all about me." They have sinned. *"The Lord saw how great man's wickedness on the earth had become; and that every inclination of the thoughts of his heart was only evil all the time. The Lord was grieved that He had made man on the earth, and His heart was filled with pain"* (vv. 5 and 6). His response was to send a great flood: *"I will wipe mankind, whom I have created, from the face of the earth..."* (v. 7). He will, in effect, destroy all of mankind—with the exception of righteous Noah and his family—and start over.

Why did God do this? Surely He is not reactive. He must have known what would happen when sin came into the world. Is "taking out" humankind a real solution for sin and selfishness? Is this how the world gets fixed? What is going on here?

Awhile back, I was having a conversation with a man who had been hurt by his brother. The relationship had become difficult. He said that he wished his brother were dead, that would make it easier. He had chosen the option of not talking to his brother, that way he could feel as though his brother was wiped out of his life. I asked him if he thought this would really fix things for him. After an initial, "Of course it does! He's out of my life!," we probed a little deeper. We talked about the flood.

Did the flood fix the sin problem? Are people now warm and fuzzy, without sin, always looking out for each other? No, of course not. But could the flood have been, among other things, God's way of showing us that wiping people out isn't the answer? Cutting people off, severing our relationships with people we don't like, isn't the fix.

The Gospel in this story is God's relationship with Noah. Verse 9 reports that Noah was righteous, blameless, and he walked with God. We can only be righteous and blameless by faith in God. Hebrews' Hall of Faith (in chapter 11) states again and again that Abraham, Enoch, and Abel lived by faith, and it was credited to them as righteousness. Hebrews 11:7 states, *"By faith Noah, when warned about things not yet seen, in holy fear built an ark to save his family. By his faith he condemned the world and became heir of the righteousness that comes by faith."*

The only way to fix the world is for God to re-enter the world in person, to live without sin and selfishness, to die for sin, and then to beat sin and evil and all of its ugliness by rising from the dead. Jesus Christ fixes the world. Our only hope for a fixed life or to fix our relationships is Jesus. The best news of all is that we have Him and all of His salvation and healing and hope through faith.

God judges evil in the world. That is clear when we read about the flood. Don't think for a moment that He is going to miss evil and not deal with it. The final Judgment Day is coming. In the meantime, wiping all people out is not the way He fixes the world. The rainbow is a sign of that promise from God. Fixing the world is always through the salvation that comes to Noah through faith. It is through the salvation that comes to us through faith in Jesus.

Lord Jesus, I have so many times felt as though You are not paying attention to the injustice and evil that I confront every day. I feel sometimes as though You want me to take matters into my own hands, to solve the problem myself, to fix things. But Your message to me is that in Jesus, You have already fixed things. I have to put my hope in Him. I have to let Him anchor my soul and desires and future. Make me like Noah—righteous, blameless, and a person who walks with You. In Jesus' name. Amen.

Questions to consider:

1. How are you trying to fix things yourself instead of trusting God for the fix? Who or what is standing in the way of your faith in God, of your walk with Him?

2. What do Hebrews 11:7 and 2 Peter 2:4-5 tell you about Noah?

3. How was Noah, "the righteous one," saved? How does that compare to the way that all people are saved?

4. How can Jesus' victory and the salvation that you have through Him help you in the challenges that you are facing right now?

Week 5: Blessed to be a Blessing!

Read Genesis 12 – The Covenant with Abraham

Social networking critics are constantly pointing out that Facebook, Twitter, and the like are making those who use them narcissistic. Some of these "experts" comment that the creators of social networking discovered our favorite website for sports, entertainment, information, and news. It is ME.com.[2] "Look what I'm doing right now." "Here's a picture of me and my latest experience." "I think this about that." "I am wearing a ..." These same "experts" called the social networking craze "the unsocial or antisocial networking craze"[3] because it literally keeps us in a bubble of our own lives with "friends" who agree with everything we say and think. We rarely have real conversations where we are challenged to think beyond ourselves, our thoughts, and our experiences. In the critics' opinion, social networking isolates us in a fantasy world.

While we may or may not agree with this assessment, isn't it interesting that human beings have the capacity to take anything good and build it around ourselves? Sin, of course, does that to us. It makes us "all about me," and that can destroy God's plan for our salvation.

God had a plan to fix the world broken by sin. He would bless the world with the Messiah, the Christ, who would live without sin, die for sin, and win victory over sin and all of its ugly consequences. God's plan would be carried out over many years through the crown of His creation—people. Genesis 12 records that God would use Abram in this plan. Abram would become the father of a great nation from which the Christ would be born. Notice God's words: *"I will bless you..."* Notice what else God says, *"...all peoples on earth will be blessed through you."* In other words, "You, Abram, are blessed to be a blessing!

---

[2] In 2008 Apple began Me.com. There was some struggle with the rollout. In 2016, Me.com became a place to store photos, files, and notes where they are safe and available. This is a lot different than the self-focused, self-absorbed practices that social networking critics referred to a decade or so ago.

[3] Numerous articles and blogs in the 2000s include this perspective. In 2011, Marc Hartzman wrote *"The Anti-Social Network: A Place For all The Thoughts, Ideas, and Plans You Don't Want to Share."*

Great things will happen to you, but it is for the good of others. It's not about you, Abram."

Abram, like us, struggled with that message. He took God's good promise and made it about himself. The last part of this chapter even finds Abram risking the plan to start a great nation through his wife, Sarai. He takes matters into his own hands and tries to protect himself and get more for himself by letting her become a part of Pharaoh's harem. God, of course, came to the rescue and set things right again.

God has blessed all of us. We have many great things in life: relationships, possessions, purpose, plans, and most of all our faith in Him. We are blessed. But do we hear His call to be a blessing? Do we consider how we might leverage what we have been given to help others? Jesus said, *"Whatever you do for the least of these...you do for me."* Ultimately, it's not about me. It's about Christ.

Lord Jesus, too often I have made my credo in life, "It's all about me." I don't like to admit it. I try to cover it up, but it is reality. Sin has made me selfish and self-centered. Forgive me. Help me to realize that You are what I am about. Help me to keep my eyes on You. Change me so that I see the blessings that You freely bestow on me as gifts to be used to bless the world. Then I will know that it is more blessed to give than to receive. In Your name I pray. Amen.

Questions to ponder:

1. What good things have you made "all about me"? How is that keeping you from blessing others?

2. Read Romans 12. How do these verses reinforce the message of Genesis 12? Notice how many times Paul tells the Romans and us not to get conceited, not to be "all about me." Why is this important to being a blessing to others?

3. How can you tap into the power of God to overcome this sin-sickness that makes us so selfish and self-focused? What spiritual disciplines can you practice that might help?

Week 6: A Father Sacrifices His Son

Read Genesis 22 – Abraham and Isaac

"God, what are You doing?"

Have you ever made that cry to God? I remember attending the funeral of a young boy who had been hit by a car and killed as he crossed the street. The mother was a wreck. A few years earlier, she had buried her 17-year-old son after a long battle with leukemia. She had just gone through a messy divorce with an alcoholic husband. She understandably cried out to God, "What are You doing?" It's not easy to understand why horrible things happen.

Abraham must have had similar thoughts. Remember that God had uprooted Abraham and his family to move to a new land so that he and his wife Sarah could have as many descendants as there are sands on the seashore. But Sarah couldn't have children. Just as couples who struggle with infertility today cry out to God, so Abraham and Sarah must have hurt and wondered about God.

Long after they had given up on God's promise to give them an abundance of descendants, God acted. At the ages of 90 and 100, long past the age of bearing children, He miraculously blessed Sarah and Abraham with a beautiful child. His name was Isaac.

We can only imagine how they loved this miracle child. They had waited so long. He was the answer to countless prayers. He was the hope of fulfilling God's promise of descendants more numerous than sands on the seashore. But then God tells Abraham to take this only child, this precious child, this child who has become the center of Abraham's universe, and sacrifice him on a mountain. "God, what are You doing?"

The story is captivating. Abraham ties Isaac to an altar. He is ready to make his son a sacrifice. God takes Abraham to the edge of killing his own son but then stops him. God provides a ram for a sacrifice to be made instead of Isaac. "God, what are You doing?"

17

We are told that this is a test to determine if Abraham loves his son Isaac more than he loves God. God commends Abraham, *"Now I know that you fear God, because you have not withheld from me your son, your only son"* (v. 12).

Did you notice that phrase that keeps repeating: *"...your son, your only son..."*?

As we notice this phrase, we realize that this story is more than a test. This story is about another Father and His only Son. This is God's story. This is our story of salvation. Isaac is like Jesus. He carries the wood for his sacrifice as Jesus carries the cross to become the ultimate sacrifice for our sin. A ram is killed. Jesus is the Lamb of God who takes away the sin of the world. The angel reiterates the promise of God to Abraham. Through Jesus' death, we are promised life everlasting. And at the heart of it all is faith.

"God so loved the world that He gave His one and only Son, that whoever believes in Him will not perish, but have everlasting life" (John 3:16).

We don't always know what God is doing, but we can rest assured that it is out of love and for our good. He is about securing our salvation. Our role: to trust Him.

Lord Jesus, I struggle with my faith sometimes. There are so many things that I don't understand. Help me to see You as the loving God that You are. Help me to realize that You did not put Abraham through more than he could bear. Keep my eyes on Jesus, the Author and Perfector of my faith. In His name I pray. Amen.

Questions to ponder:

1. What has happened in your life that caused you to ask: "God, what are You doing?"

2. What good did God work in that situation? Were you faithful? Did your faith grow? How can seeing what good God did help you in future struggles?

3. What verses from the Bible do you lean on during these times? Make a list and make sure that you have committed them to memory. Here are some suggestions: Romans 8:28, 38-39; Hebrews 12:7-11; Matthew 6:25-34.

4. How might your experiences help you to help others who go through difficult times? Who do you need to help right now?

Week 7: When God Interrupts

Read Exodus 3 – The Call of Moses

There I was, right in the middle of preparing a sermon. My mind was deep in thought as I studied the text of Scripture...when the phone rang. At first, I didn't want to answer. Sometimes, it takes a while to get started and, as I get older, I have noticed that an interruption can cause me to lose not only my train of thought but the whole thought. So I reasoned, "It's probably just a salesperson. I'm on a roll. It'd be great to get this written now." Still, in the back of my mind, the persistent reminder echoed, "The phone is ringing; someone might need some help." I relented and picked up the phone to hear the crying voice of a young wife who had just discovered some ugly news about her husband—news that was threatening their marriage. God interrupted. He used me to help. But at first, it wasn't an easy transition for me.

Can you relate to the struggle when God interrupts?

Consider Moses. He was going about the business of marriage and supporting a family when God showed up and interrupted. Moses was out in the wilderness when, from a burning bush, God told him that He wanted Moses to change the course of what he was doing. God wanted Moses to confront the most powerful man in the world (the Pharaoh of Egypt), convince him to let go of his slave force (God's people, the Israelites), and lead His people out of slavery in Egypt to the "promised land." This interruption was far more significant than a phone call. This was about the plan of salvation. This would change the course of Moses' life. This would be a lifelong change.

Is it any wonder that Moses struggled with this change of events, this interruption? Does it surprise us at all that Moses began to question God, question his own ability, and want to get out of the interruption?

Ever wonder what would've happened if Moses would not have answered God's call? What would have happened if Moses would have walked right by that burning bush?

For Moses, there would have been no confronting the most powerful leader in the world and watching him wilt under the power of God during the ten plagues. There would have been no awesome parting of the Red Sea or receiving of the Ten Commandments from God Himself. He would not have experienced manna or quail in the wilderness. Of course, Moses would not have had to deal with the complaining of the people or the wandering in the wilderness for 40 years, but think of what he would've missed if he had not let God interrupt him.

Sometimes we think that interruptions will wreck things for us, but God was not trying to ruin the life of Moses or his family. God only had in mind the future of all humankind. He wanted to use Moses in His great plan of salvation. He wanted to align Moses with the real plan for Moses' life—God's plan—so that Moses would not miss his appointment with God (would not be "dis"-appointed).

Maybe we should start looking for the interruptions of God instead of trying to avoid them. Maybe we should be praying more for God to align us with His plan for our lives, His great plan for salvation.

Lord Jesus, sometimes I am so busy trying to get my business accomplished that I forget about Your business. Don't let me be so consumed by what I consider to be the urgent stuff of life that I miss the important stuff of life. You have saved me to be a blessing to the world. Use me in the big things and the little things of life to help Your Kingdom come. Remove my excuses and hesitancy. Give me courage to act for You. In Jesus' name I pray. Amen.

Questions to ponder:

1. What are you praying that God would use you to do in and for His Kingdom?

2. What do the following verses teach you about being ready to serve God?

- Hebrews 13:1-2

- 1 Peter 1:13-22

- 1 Peter 3:15

- 1 Corinthians 12:1-7

3. Can you think of a time when God interrupted you? How did you respond? What lessons will help you to answer God's call the next time He interrupts?

Week 8: The Lamb

Read Exodus 12 – Passover

The battle between God (Yahweh) and Pharaoh (who considered himself to be a god) built to a climax as each plague wreaked its havoc. After each terrible judgment, the hard heart of the Pharaoh would soften—yet, when he escaped from the threat, he arrogantly refused to free the people. Finally, the worst of all plagues was set in motion. This would not be slimy frogs or pesky swarms of flies or locusts. This plague would include death itself—the killing of the firstborn.

For Egyptians and Hebrews, the firstborn was viewed as sacred. Perhaps more than any other occurrence in the life of a married couple, the birth of the first child was miraculous. And for the farmer or for the one who raised livestock, the first fruit and the firstborn were unique. The tenth plague was the worst because it struck at the very heart of Egyptian and Hebrew culture unless...the blood of a lamb was smeared on the doorposts of a home. *"The blood will be a sign for you on the houses where you are; and when I see the blood, I will pass over you. No destructive plague will touch you when I strike Egypt"* (Exodus 12:13).

Sin strikes at the very heart of our culture. It destroys community as it creates walls and isolates. It devastates the human spirit as it looks out only for self, leaving us feeling unloved and unwanted. It drives us toward despair as it discourages and fosters fear and anxiety. It is toxic. It is death. Sin kills.

And sin is rampant. It touches us all. Jesus said, *"Flesh gives birth to flesh"* (John 3). Sinful people have sinful kids. We don't have to be taught to do selfish, sinful things; it comes naturally. So does its consequence: death. Just as both Egyptian and Hebrew could experience the horrid consequences of the killing of the firstborn, so all people are touched by death. We have to die. Our loved ones have to die, and death is ugly.

I remember helping some friends in their forties walk through the cancer experience. She had breast cancer—the aggressive kind. What a roller coaster of questions, pain, hope, and fear. In this case, the "ride" ended in the hospital. As her husband and I held her hands, she took her last gasps of life. He broke our silence and commented, "That was ugly. I wouldn't wish that on anybody."

But there is deliverance. There is victory. There is the Lamb. For the Hebrews who would listen, there was the Passover Lamb: *"Tell the whole community of Israel that on the tenth day of this month each man is to take a lamb..."* (Exodus 12:3). For us, it is the Lamb of God, Jesus, who takes away the sin of the world. They sacrificed a lamb that was a year old without defect. For us, it is Jesus, the perfect (without defect) Son of God. They slaughtered the lamb at twilight. Jesus was crucified on the cross on Good Friday, dying near the end of the day. They smeared the blood on the doorposts of their houses with hyssop. We have the blood of the Lamb of God smeared on our hearts by the Holy Spirit through faith. They were saved from death as the angel passed over their homes. We are saved from spiritual and eternal death as God helps us to pass through the valley of the shadow of death and receive life here and hereafter.

For the people of the first Exodus and for people today, the key is the Lamb. It is only by Him, in Him, and through Him that we are saved.

Lord Jesus, You are the Lamb of God who takes away the sins of the world. Thank You for working faith in my heart so that I might have victory over death, so that I might live with and for You. In Jesus' powerful name I pray. Amen.

Questions to ponder:

1. Read Hebrews 12:2. Are your eyes fixed on Jesus? What distracts you the most?

2. Are you totally relying on Jesus for your salvation, or do you have thoughts that it is because you are good or haven't done anything heinous? Memorize Ephesians 2:8-9.

3. Read Ephesians 6:10-18. Here Paul talks about the battle against this dark world. How do Paul's words compare with the battle that raged between God and Pharaoh? What does God give you for the battles in your life? Describe this armor that applies to your life.

Week 9: Be Still!

Read Exodus 14 – Red Sea Deliverance

They were trapped, cornered, doomed. Or so they thought. What to do?

After the plague of the first-born, God's people, the Israelites, were free—free from slavery, free to worship the True God. They left Egypt quickly, before the Pharaoh would change his mind, and journeyed toward Mount Sinai where God would give them the Ten Commandments. God accompanied them in a pillar of cloud by day and a pillar of fire by night, and Moses led them to camp by the Red Sea. (A pillar of cloud by day and a pillar of fire by night...Wouldn't that be nice—to know visibly that God was present as you journey through life?)

But their greatest fears were realized as the Pharaoh changed his mind. He took 600 of his best chariots, their officers, and many other chariots and pursued the Israelites, finally catching up to them as they camped by the Red Sea. The people were terrified. The greatest army from the greatest nation in the world was on one side. The Red Sea was on the other.

So, what did they do? They complained. They blamed. They went after Moses, "Why didn't you leave us in Egypt?" They attacked God, "It would have been better for us to be slaves than to die." None of this made any sense to them. "What have you done to us?"

Research of the human brain indicates that we have a higher brain that analyzes and reflects and creates. We think. We also have a lower brain; some call it reptilian. This is where automatic processes occur that are not about thinking but surviving. This reptilian brain reacts, fights, or runs. When trapped by the Egyptians, this is the part of the brain that was stimulated to terror and fear. While the lower brain may save us with its "fight or flight" two-choice reaction, it does not allow us to think and respond to God and His presence. Brain experts tell us that the chemical mix (adrenaline, etc.) that our lower brain releases into our body actually keeps us from connecting to our higher brain for about fifteen minutes (or more).

It is at this time that Moses says, *"Do not be afraid...The Lord will fight for you; you need only to be still."* Psalm 46:10 puts it this way: "Be still and know that I am God."

Can you relate to the Israelite reaction when feeling trapped? If you have truly experienced a time when you thought your family might break apart, your job might be lost, a loved one died, you got a bad diagnosis, or your child or parent made a bad choice, most likely you can relate. At such times, we react. It's either fight or flight or we are paralyzed. Fear becomes an overwhelming force that controls our actions and words and thoughts.

God's advice? Be still. Do nothing. Give yourself some time to settle down. Let your higher brain re-engage and then start praying. God has been there all along. Go to Him and give Him your anxiety (1 Peter 5:7) and questions and confusion. Let Him be God, which means let Him take care of the situation. That's what faith is.

It's amazing that the Israelites forgot the pillar of cloud and the pillar of fire, God's presence right in front of them. It's amazing that they had forgotten the power of God exhibited in the Ten Plagues. We would think that God would be impatient with them for their forgetfulness. But that is not the case at all. He loves them and delivers them with another miracle: the parting of the Red Sea. With water, He wipes out their enemy and frees them to live for Him. They will carry this miracle with them for the rest of their lives. They really can have faith in Him.

In the same way, with water in Baptism, God wipes out our enemy: sin. We are free to live for Him. This miracle is one that we carry with us for the rest of our time here and hereafter into eternity. This miracle is what we tune into when we are still. We don't have to be reptilian. We can trust in a loving God. We really can have faith in Him.

Lord Jesus, there are times when I feel as though I am up against it. Fear, doubt, and confusion threaten me. In those times, help me to "be still and know that You are God." Help me to remember the waters of Baptism through which I am saved from my enemy: sin. May I always see Your loving presence around me and live in victory for You. In Jesus' powerful name I pray. Amen.

Questions to consider:

1. Can you name some verses that you lean on when times get tough in your life? Ask other Christians what verses they use in trying times. If you haven't already, commit them to memory.

2. Read Luke 10:38-42. Contrast the actions of Mary and Martha. What do you think caused Martha to be so busy? What causes you to be so busy? Even more important, how does that busyness keep you from living in the Lord?

3. We are often captive to our feelings. In other words, we can know the right thing to do, but because we feel fear, anxiety, guilt, or insecurity so strongly, we aren't able to "be still and let God be God." What is your weakness? What is your default (what you tend to do under stress)? Take it to the Lord in prayer.

Week 10: The Benefit of Boundaries

Read Exodus 20 – Ten Commandments

In his landmark book, <u>Boundaries</u>,[4] Dr. John Townsend says, "Boundaries are one's personal property line. They are how you define yourself, say who you are and who you are not, set limits, and establish consequences." What would a basketball game be without boundaries? How would we know what a touchdown or home run were without the boundary of a goal line or a foul pole? How could we be accident free on the highway without the yellow line that runs down the middle of the road? Boundaries can be very good for us.

As God's people left Egypt, they had great confusion as to who they were and how they were to live. They had been living in a pagan world, influenced by a secular culture for generation after generation. How were they to worship the true God? What place did He have in their everyday lives? How were they to respond to authorities like parents and government? How should they handle their emotions, sexuality, and property in a God-pleasing way? What about desires? We all have them. Are they wrong? What about sanctity of life issues? God's people did not have a Bible on their phone or on their coffee table. They had major questions.

It is in this context that God spoke to them about love and life. He loves them and has just saved them through the spilling of the blood of the first-born. They have been set free as a result of the Passover and Red Sea experiences. He wants them now to live life to its fullest. Out of this great love, He speaks into their lives the Decalogue that we call the Ten Commandments. Out of love, God defines His people and real living. He cares so much about them that He can't just leave them wandering in a fog about who they are and, more importantly, *whose* they are.

How do you view the Ten Commandments? Are they an obligation that creates a barrier between you and God? Are they a burden? Are they a suggestion about a better way to live? Are they an impossible-to-accomplish to-do list?

---

[4] <u>Boundaries</u>, Dr. Henry Cloud & Dr. John Townsend, Zondervan, 1992.

There was a study done of students playing outside on a playground. The playground was fenced; it had a boundary. As a result, the children felt safe and enjoyed the entire playground area. When the boundary (the fence) was removed, the children hovered near the center of the playground around the swings and slide. They didn't experience and enjoy the expanse of the playground.

Could it be that the Ten Commandments are God's boundary for our lives? Could it be that they provide clarity and safety, that they are a great blessing to us?

Jesus said in His Sermon on the Mount that when He came *"...not the smallest letter, not the least stroke of a pen, will by any means disappear from the Law..."* (Matthew 5:18). Apparently, God cares so much for us that He does not want us to wander in the fog of an increasingly pagan, secular culture. He wants us to experience life in all of its fullness and joy. He wants to define who He is and how we are to live. He wants to tell us about the wonder of life, its sanctity, and that we are not to intervene at the beginning of life or at the end of it. He wants to tell us about the beauty of marriage and family, that marriage is between one man and one woman and is meant to last a lifetime. He wants to teach us about desiring good things that come from Him while trusting Him to take care of all of our needs. He wants to teach us to respect others, loving them as we love ourselves, not letting our selfishness or emotions or attitudes get in the way of that love.

Most of all, Jesus wants us to know that by ourselves we cannot obey these commandments or live within their boundaries. Life, as He defines it, true life, is only possible in a relationship with Him. That's because He is the only human being who understood and lived these Commandments perfectly. When He died on the cross, it was because we mess up and sin. It was to give us His perfection and power for living life the way it was created to be lived. Jesus is the perfect obedience of the Commandments. That perfect obedience is ours through faith in Him.

Can the Commandments be overwhelming? Yes, without a doubt. But they were given by God out of love. Obedience to them is secured by God through the loving sacrifice of Jesus. We have the boundaries of real living that were given and secured by our Lord and Savior. So let's live it up obeying the Commandments, living within God's boundaries, with great joy!

Lord Jesus, thank You for loving me so much that You would give me boundaries. Thank You for parents and authorities that reinforce and teach those boundaries. Help me to realize that my obedience to these Commandments is what real living is all about. Give me the righteousness of Jesus because I cannot obey on my own. Keep me faithful to You, my eyes fixed on Jesus. In His name I pray. Amen.

Questions to consider:

1. Read Mark 12:30-31 and note the two commandments that Jesus gives. Align the Ten Commandments with the two commandments of Jesus.

2. Some have said that the Lord's Prayer is a prayer to obey the Ten Commandments. Match the petitions of the Lord's Prayer with the Commandments. Do you see the alignment?

3. How does Romans 12:2 challenge us to live the Ten Commandments? What power and advice does this verse offer?

4. Persistence in living for God is one of our greatest challenges. How do Galatians 6:9 and Matthew 11:28 help?

Week 11: God is Present!

Read Exodus 40 - Tabernacle

Where is God When it Hurts?[5] is a best-selling book written by Philip Yancey in response to the question that many ask in the face of pain and difficulty. Maybe you have wondered in the midst of a tragedy or setback if God really cares, if He really is present. Sometimes we can't help but wonder.

The word *dwell* (Exodus 25:8) has a specific meaning. In the Hebrew language, it is the same word as that used for a tabernacle. It's a little like our modern word *tent*. It could be used as a noun or a verb. As God instructs the building of the Tabernacle, He is not just talking about a structure (tent). He is really telling His people what He is doing. His activity was and is to tabernacle (dwell) in the center of His people. He is providing a visible presence as they wander through the wilderness.

It is as if God knows that we need a physical presence from Him. During their exodus, the people of Israel had that presence from God in the form of a pillar of cloud by day and a pillar of fire by night. But that wouldn't always be the case. Beginning in Exodus 25, God tells them to build a Tabernacle. He gives them specific instructions for its location among the people: in the center of the camp. He tells them what to put in the Tabernacle: the Ark of the Covenant (with the tablets of stone on which the Ten Commandments were written), the Table, the Lampstand, and other pieces. He identifies the materials used to build these pieces. He gives them the dimensions of the courtyard and the Tabernacle that is within it. They need a place that will be full of details and activities that will teach them about God's character and will, about how they can relate to Him, come to Him, no matter what is happening in their lives.

In the Gospel of John, we are told, *"In the beginning was the Word and the Word was with God and the Word was God."* In verse 14 John reveals, *"The Word became flesh and made His dwelling (tabernacle) among us. We*

---

[5] Where is God When It Hurts, by Philip Yancey, originally published in 1977.

have seen His glory, the glory of the One and Only..." Every Jew recognized that phrase: "...made His dwelling among us." It referenced the Tabernacle that became the Temple, which was the physical presence of God.

Where is God when it hurts? The Tabernacle and Temple are now destroyed, but God is present. He is dwelling with us as the Word, Jesus. He is present in the Word. No wonder God is always calling us to read the Bible, which gives us great comfort and direction. He is present in the bread and wine of the Sacrament of the Altar and tells us "...do this often in remembrance of Me."

Sometimes when we hurt, we move away from God. We feel as if He has left us. As we return to the tangible places (the Bible and His Supper) where we know that He tabernacles among us, we discover not only His presence but His healing and strength.

Lord God Almighty, sometimes I am absolutely certain that You are present. I look at the heavens or the beauty of creation, and You are there. I attend worship, and Your Spirit is palpable. Other times, I struggle. I wonder whether You are interested in me and my problems. I wonder if You are real. Forgive me for my times of doubt. Help me in my unbelief (Mark 9:24). Help me to know that You are present always. Keep me walking in step with You as I worship and read Your Word. In Your name I pray. Amen.

Questions to consider:

1. Name a time when you have felt far from God or as though He was not present. What did you do to overcome this? What would you do differently? Memorize some passages that remind you of God's presence (such as Matthew 28:20b or Hebrews 13:5).

2. Read 2 Chronicles 5:13-14, 2 Chronicles 7:19-21, 2 Kings 25, Haggai 2:6-9, and Ezekiel 10:1-22. What happened to the presence of God in the Tabernacle and then the Temple?

3. God's Temple was rebuilt in 516 B.C. and then again later by King Herod. God's Son, Jesus, became His dwelling place on this earth for a while. What happened to that dwelling place (Acts 1:1-11)? Note the use of a cloud and think back to the presence of God during the Exodus.

Week 12: Sin Requires a Savior!

Read Leviticus 16 – The Day of Atonement

What does sin do to us?
- Do you realize that it makes us sick? Sad? Anxious? Afraid? Guilty?
- Do you know that sin breaks relationships? Prompts deceit? Causes violence? Seduces to immorality? Destroys values?
- Do you realize that sin kills—here and hereafter?
- Do you realize sin keeps you from intimacy with God?

Sin is serious, so what are we going to do about it?

The answer is nothing! We can do nothing to get rid of sin. Our only hope is God—thus, the Day of Atonement.

One day each year, year after year, the whole community of God's people would stop. Nobody worked. Nobody ate. They stopped everything and came together for cleansing from sin—a time of new beginning. Imagine the people of Israel gathered around the courtyard. Everybody is watching. Then Aaron, the high priest, begins to offer a sacrifice to atone for his own sin, because he is a sinner just like everybody else.

Next, Aaron prepares to make a sacrifice for all the people. He takes the blood from that sacrifice and goes into the Most Holy Place to sprinkle the blood on the atonement cover on the Ark of the Covenant. While in the Most Holy Place, all the people stand outside waiting. Some are praying. Some are crying. Some are explaining to their children what is happening. All are deeply aware of why Aaron has gone to the Most Holy Place. They are sinners, and he is there to deal with their sins. On this Day of Atonement, everybody remembers their sin.

The crowd is filled with people like you and me—selfish people who revolve around their own lives, people who manipulate and control others, people too busy for God, people whose marriages are falling apart, people who struggle with sexual sins, parents who are not patient with their children, greedy people, people with every sin imaginable. They stand and wait. Will he come back soon? Is everything alright? Will God show up? Is God still with them even though they struggle with sin? Can they truly be forgiven? These and countless other questions are swirling in their heads.

When Aaron returns from the Most Holy Place, he takes another animal, a goat, chosen by chance. He places his hands on the goat's head and confesses the sins of all the people. This goes on for some time. As Aaron does this, the people think of their sins. Then the scapegoat is sent away. *"The goat will carry on itself all their sins to a solitary place and the man shall release it in the wilderness"* (Lev. 16:22).

Finally, the people can breathe again. All is well. They have been reminded of their forgiveness for another year. Year after year, the Day of Atonement is experienced. Generations of people are born, live, sin, confess, and die. God is taking care of their sin.

Atone in the Hebrew language means to cover. These sacrifices will cover their sins so that they can be "at one" (united) with God again. That's why they had to come back to the temple year after year.[6]

Thousands of years later, we have One who takes away sin—not through a lamb or goat but through the sacrifice of His life. The sacrifice of Jesus, the perfect Lamb of God, was horrid because sin is horrid; yet, it is once and for all—final! Sin is separated from us as far as the east is from the west (Psalm 102). No more Day of Atonement is needed. Jesus is our Savior.

What are we going to do about our sin? Confess it and take it to Jesus.

Lord Jesus, I come to You right now with my sins. You are the Son of God. You are perfect. You never made a mistake. That's why Your sacrifice can be once and for all—for me. Forgive my sins. Take them away. I don't want them or their ugly consequences. I want to live for You here and with You forever. I want to be "at one" with You. Thank You for the forgiveness I have through faith. In Your powerful name I pray. Amen.

---

[6] The description of the Day of Atonement in this devotion is from <u>Old Testament Challenge 1: Creating a New Community</u> - Teaching Guide; Zondervan; 2003; pages 134-135.

Questions to consider:

1. It is always helpful to name your sins before God. Spend some time getting specific with your sins. Keep in mind that God loves you and wants to convict you of your sins so that He can forgive your sin and keep it from blocking your relationship with Him.

2. Read Hebrews 10:1-18. Compare this to the Leviticus 16 account you have read.

3. Matthew 27:50-51 states that at Jesus' death, the curtain through which one entered the Most Holy Place was torn from top to bottom. What does this mean for you and your relationship with God?

4. Read Hebrews 10:19-25 and note the way you can now live since Christ Jesus has made this sacrifice once and for all.

Week 13: Cold-Water Christians

Palm Sunday, the week before Easter
Read Psalm 118 – Give Thanks

"Mom and Dad, I want to be a marine biologist. I want to go to college and get a job working with dolphins." The parents listened carefully but were not in favor of this dream. They knew that their resources were limited. They thought that the job market would be extremely tight. They were afraid. "No, you cannot go to college if this is your major. We won't allow it." The daughter was devastated. Cold water had been poured on her dream.

St. Paul tells us, *"Do not quench the Spirit's fire..."* (1 Thessalonians 5:19). Don't pour cold water on the Spirit's dream to empower people to praise and proclaim Jesus to the ends of the earth. Paul precedes these words with, "Be joyful always; pray continually; give thanks in all circumstances..." These are acts of worship and praise. These actions keep our hearts, minds, and lives focused on Jesus. Praise, prayer, and thanksgiving help keep us from being a part of the "cold-water committee" in our family, at our church, and even within our own heart. Could this be one of the prime reasons why God invites us into constant and consistent worship?

Psalm 118 is a song of worship. It is full of praise. It starts with thanksgiving; *"...for God is good, His love endures forever."*

Doubt pours cold water on the Spirit's fire. Thanksgiving requires remembering, and remembering the acts and attributes of God drives away doubt. Remembering the history of God's presence and love in answer to my cries of anguish dispels our doubts.

Fear pours cold water on the Spirit's fire. Whether or not we attempt to understand or control our fear, it still effectively quenches the dreams of the Spirit for our life. In the Word and in worship, we are reminded that the perfect love of God drives out fear (1 John 4:18). Praise God! Give thanks! *"The Lord is with me; I will not be afraid. What can man do to me?"*

Disobedience pours cold water on the Spirit's fire. When we turn from God's desire for our life, the Spirit is grieved. His hopes and dreams for us are sidetracked. In worship we repent, literally letting Him turn our life around—away from our enemies, sin, and Satan—and back to Him and His will for my life. *"The Lord is with me; He is my helper. I will look in triumph on my enemies."*

Failure pours cold water on the Spirit's fire. We remember. We give thanks. We praise God that when *"I was pushed back and about to fall, the Lord helped me. The Lord is my strength and my song..."* Worship and praise of the resurrected Jesus move me away from my tendency to define myself by my failures instead of His victory.

Death pours cold water on the Spirit's fire. Since death is a reality, we can easily develop a grab-for-all-I-can way of living that blocks God's eternal desire for our life. But our God is not held or held up by death. In worship, *"Shouts of joy and victory resound in the tents of the righteous."* The Lord's right hand has triumphed.

During the week before Easter (Holy Week), we walk with Jesus as He makes the ultimate love sacrifice for our sin. We have been redeemed. We have been freed to live a new life for Him. He has dreams for us that have eternal implications. *"I will not die but live, and will proclaim what the Lord has done...Give thanks to the Lord, for He is good; His love endures forever."*

Lord Jesus Christ, forgive me for quenching the Spirit's plan for my life. Remind me of the benefits of worship—prayer, praise, and giving thanks. May I never forget the love that You have for me and the victory that You have won for me. Keep my eyes on Jesus so that I may live for Him. In His powerful name I pray. Amen.

Questions to consider:

1. Read Ephesians 2:8-9. Now read Ephesians 2:10. The Greek word translated *workmanship* is one that suggests that Jesus saved us so that our lives would be a Spirit-designed poem. Take a pen and paper and begin to pray about and write your poem.

2. Are you dousing the Spirit's dreams for your life with cold water? Make a list of cold-water habits, attitudes, and emotions that keep you from living the life God has prepared for you. Confess them and receive God's forgiveness for them. Talk to a close family member or friend to help you develop a plan for addressing these cold-water tendencies.

3. Make a list of the promises of Psalm 118 for which you can give thanks to God. Think about how these promises keep you from quenching the Spirit's fire.

Week 14: Running toward the Resurrection!
Easter Week
Read John 20 – The Resurrection of Jesus

A group of kids had just finished a game of soccer. It was hot, and their red faces and slumped shoulders revealed that they were exhausted. Then, one of the dads yelled, "Who wants ice cream?" Suddenly, filled with energy, they ran to get their treat.

"There's been a bad accident on the school playground," someone told a group of mothers at coffee. Without hesitation, every one of them jumped up and started running toward the school.

Isn't it interesting that we run toward both good news and bad news? We must know, and quickly, if the news—good or bad—relates to us.

Take a look at the Easter story according to John. There sure is a lot of running on that day. Mary Magdalene came running to Simon Peter. *"They've taken away my Lord and I don't know where to find Him,"* she shouts (v. 13). Is this good news or bad news? Peter and the other disciple hear her words and start running to the tomb. In fact, it seems like they are in a race. What are they running toward? Is there good news or bad news at the tomb? What does this empty tomb mean for their future?

Do you run toward the resurrection? Or do you run away from it? Or, maybe even worse, are you running around so fast that you actually never really think of the resurrection and its implications for your life?

The resurrection can certainly be a challenge for people to believe. Mary had to see the Lord and hear His voice. Thomas needed to touch the wounds on Jesus' hands and feet and side. He needed evidence. The other disciples needed Jesus' presence. Jesus said, *"Because you have seen Me, you have believed; blessed are those who have not seen and yet have believed"* (v. 29). That is our generation—the ones who are blessed to believe even though we haven't seen in person the resurrected Christ. Are we like the other disciple, the "disciple Jesus loved," who did not see Jesus (only the empty tomb) and believed (v. 8)?

Believing, no matter how difficult, causes us to run **toward** the resurrection. We are to keep our eyes on Jesus. We have a faith relationship with the One who beat sin and death and the devil. We have the Victorious Christ. We are truly alive as we love God with all our heart, soul, mind, and strength. We experience life in all of its abundance when we love others as we love ourselves. The same is true as we celebrate and experience His creation here and anticipate the future that we have in heaven after finally grasping victory over death.

God makes this believing possible through His Holy Spirit. He enables us, who live millennia away from the time of the resurrection, to "see" the risen Christ. He does that in the Bible where He reminds us that these things are written *"...that you may believe that Jesus is the Christ, the Son of God, and that by believing you may have life in His name"* (v. 31).

Lord Jesus, forgive me for my tendency to run away from the resurrection and its ramifications for my life. Forgive me for the times I have been running so fast after the things of this world that I have missed the meaning of the resurrection. Help me to run toward the victory that Jesus Christ has won. Make my life a living testimony of the new life that He gives through faith. In Your powerful name I pray. Amen.

Thoughts to consider:

1. How do you think Mary Magdalene was feeling on resurrection day? Notice the language that Jesus uses as He speaks to her? What does He call the disciples in verse 17? How is all of this so reassuring to her?

2. How many times, according to John, does Jesus say, "Peace be with you" in verses 19-26? How does this relate to the disciples' fears? Your fears?

3. Thomas doubted, but at least he did believe. Who are you most like in the John 20 account? Thomas? Mary? Simon? The "other disciple"? Remember that Jesus loved them all, and they were used in a powerful way.

4. Read at least one of the other Gospel accounts of the resurrection and compare it to John 20 (Matthew 28; Mark16; Luke 24). What are the similarities? What are the differences?

   • Similarities:

   • Differences:

5. What is the wonderful message that God is communicating in all four of the resurrection accounts?

Week 15: When People Mistreat God

Read Psalm 2 – A Messianic Psalm

Have you ever been upset because you heard someone continually curse using God's name in vain? Have you ever wanted to shut someone up as they go on and on that God is not the Creator or that He doesn't even exist? Do you ever get absolutely frustrated when you watch a professing Christian offend God by living totally contrary to His will? I remember an arrogant coworker who set me off in this way. I wanted God to set him straight. I wanted him to understand his flawed thinking. I wanted him to "see the light." Sad to say, as far as I know, he never did get it about God.

Most scholars think that Psalm 2 was composed for the coronation of a king. Often a new king was crowned at a time of revolt and challenge. Not everyone inside and outside of the nation necessarily agreed who should be king. There was plotting and scandal, all aimed at undermining the one who would be king.

When we read this Psalm carefully, we quickly notice that it is less about an earthly king and more about the ultimate King—Jesus Christ. Therefore, the Psalm includes a sharp contrast between those who challenge the Lord's Anointed One and God's response to that challenge.

Notice that "they" conspire, plot, and take stands against God. They put up road blocks and prevent people from seeing God for Who He is. They promise a freedom from God that—like fish free from the water or a tree free from the soil—is no freedom at all, only death. They are like the hypocritical people that upset and frustrate us.

Notice even more that God is not daunted or impaired by their actions. They don't threaten Him one iota. They don't change His plans or Who He is. In fact, He laughs at them. He rebukes them. He terrifies them. Nothing, absolutely nothing gets in the way of His eternal love for people and His desire to save the world through the Anointed One—His Son, King Jesus.

Consider the plan of salvation when Jesus came to earth and died on the cross. Nothing stopped God's story. Consider the second coming of Jesus as described in Revelation and throughout the Bible. Nothing stands against God and His final judgment of evil and those who are promoters of it.

While it is important for us to defend the Christian faith, while it is necessary to have an answer to the challenges that people bring against God, He does not need our defense. He is all-powerful and all-loving. Jesus' offer of salvation cannot be compromised. *"Blessed are all who take refuge in Him"* (v. 12).

Lord Jesus Christ, You are the King of Kings and Lord of Lords. Help me to rest assured that even though there is evil all around me, even though it feels like this world is unraveling at an alarming rate, You are victorious. Nothing stopped Your trek to the cross, and nothing will keep me from the salvation You have won for me and all the world. Help me to take refuge in You. In Jesus' name I pray. Amen.

Questions to ponder:

1. Which words about God and His Anointed comfort you the most in this psalm?

2. The New Testament frequently applies this psalm to Jesus. Consider Matthew 3:17, Acts 4:25-27, Acts 13:33, Hebrews 1:5, and Hebrews 5:5. To what verse in the psalm do each of these New Testament verses refer? What do they teach you about Jesus?

3. How do you feel God deals with you? An iron rod? Pottery for repair? A kiss? A flare up? Remember that in Jesus, your sins are forgiven.

Week 16: Passing the Torch of Faith

Read Deuteronomy 6 – "Hear, O Israel..." (Shema)

One of the more startling statistics concerning Christianity is that less than 25%[7] of people in their 20s are actively living their faith in Jesus Christ. When my wife and I became parents in the 1980s, one of our primary goals was to make sure that our kids knew and loved Jesus Christ. Probably most Christian parents begin the parenting journey that way. So, what happens? Where do we go wrong? Do we get distracted by other goals? Do we get tired of fighting against non-Christian and even anti-Christian messages in our culture? Do we become afraid that we will lose our relationship with our children when they start neglecting God's guidance for their lives or rebelling against God and faith?

The purpose here is not to criticize parents too harshly; the task of raising Christ-following children is overwhelming. Sin gets in the way in both parents and children. Sometimes, even with the best parenting, a child leaves the Christian faith.

The Bible and, especially, Deuteronomy 6 lay out a plan of action that includes some core principles, habits, and characteristics that parents can teach and model:
1. Faith in Christ is formed by the power of the Holy Spirit in personal, trusted relationships within the family. Therefore, do whatever possible to build a strong parent-child relationship.
2. The local church is in a living partnership with families to help in passing the torch of faith.
3. Where Christ is present in faith, the home is also the church, so make home a place where children learn about Jesus and His love.
4. Faith is caught (modeled) as much as it is taught.
5. Children with strong faith have parents with strong faith in Jesus. Growing faith is important in parents as well as in children.

There are also some key habits for passing the torch of faith. These can help any parent. They include: caring conversations (talking with love about Jesus and His church); devotions (these can be in the car, at

---

[7] Pew Research 2017

meals, or whenever); service (parents taking children with them to help someone because we love Jesus, followed by a conversation about the serving experience); rituals and traditions like holidays centered in Jesus Christ or vacations with some learning about Christ. Habits like these are remembered for a lifetime by our children.

Finally, as we practice these principles and habits, pray that God will bless us to live like Jesus, reflecting Christian characteristics. First is authenticity. This means being honest about personal doubts and faith questions, making sure that actions match words. Second, be available. The only way that children will truly learn and grow is if we are present as parents to teach and model the faith. This is a daily opportunity that begins when children are young. It has to be a high priority all the time. Third, affirm and encourage. It is so important that children know how much Jesus loves them and how much we love them.[8]

The Bible is clear that God has given us children as a wonderful gift. It is also clear that He loves them and wants to be in relationship with them. May we be strengthened in our faith so that we might pass it on to a young one in the faith.

Lord Jesus, help me to see that I am privileged to share Your salvation with others, especially the young people in my life. Help me to see the opportunities You put around me. Bless my efforts to pass the torch of faith to the next generation. In Jesus' name I pray. Amen.

Questions to consider:

1. What words of this chapter encourage you in the task of passing the torch of faith?

---

[8] The principles, habits, and modeling characteristics in this devotion are spoken of in the book, Frogs without Legs Can't Hear: Nurturing Discipleship in Home and Congregation, by David W. Anderson and Rev. Paul Hill; Augsburg Fortress; published in 2003.

2. What is the message that has to be passed to the next generation? How does God want the next generation to live their faith?

3. Who is someone that you can pass the torch of faith to? What specific things can you do to help that person? Make a plan of action.

   • Action plan (who, what, where, when, how):

4. The *Shema* was a prayer taught and repeated every day. What does that remind us about the nature of passing the torch of faith? Make sure your plan of action from #3 includes a consistent, reminding habit.

Week 17: Bucket List
Read Joshua 24 – Covenant Renewal

A bucket list includes the things a person wants to accomplish or experience before one dies. A list might include: going deep sea fishing or to the Super Bowl, witnessing an eclipse or St. Peter's Cathedral in Rome, learning to salsa dance or speak French. Usually, these activities are about personal dreams or goals. They rarely have to do with influencing others or making a difference for the good.

Joshua has lived a long life. He's wandered in the wilderness, led a miraculous crossing of the Jordan river, fought great battles in places like Jericho, seen the sun stand still, and established God's people in the Promised Land. That's enough to fill any bucket list. Now he comes to the end of his life and what does he do?

Joshua assembles all of the people of God (the twelve tribes of Israel), the elders, leaders, judges, and officials. He presents them before the Lord and then renews the covenant that God has made with them. He lists the history of God's faithfulness first to Abraham, then to Moses, and finally to them. He reminds them of God's blessings of land and food and victory. God has kept His part of the covenant. Now, they must be faithful to Him. "Fear Him. Serve Him, not false, pagan gods. Serve the true God." Joshua leads the people in a pledge of allegiance to God. They repeat the typical language and ritual of a covenant. They pledge their faithfulness to the God of Abraham, Isaac, and Jacob; the God of the Red Sea, Ten Commandments, and the Tabernacle; the holy, jealous God who loves them and forgives them and blesses them.

Can you see yourself at the end of your days visiting with all of your friends to ensure that they are committed to God? Can you imagine gathering your kids and grandkids around your death-bed for the purpose of telling them that the most important thing in life is to stay faithful to the God who faithfully sent His Son to the cross? Moses did it. Paul did it. Joshua does it. It really isn't a bad idea for a bucket list.

Better yet! Why not add to our bucket list a commitment to tell all our family members about Jesus and His love for them right now? Instead of putting it at the end of our life, begin today...way before we die. If we want to do something really big, add to that list telling friends and neighbors our story of life with God. Some people never get their bucket list finished. Touching lives with Jesus' love is too important to wait until our last days.

With a bucket list, we check off an item and are done. Think about it: those experiences like sky diving, bungee jumping, or traveling to New Zealand will be remembered for a while by a picture on the wall or a video in your drawer. The kinds of things that Joshua was doing have lifelong benefits and last forever. The spreading of the Good News of Jesus needs to be a perpetual item on our bucket list.

Lord Jesus, thank You for Your faithfulness to me. You kept Your promise to save the world by sacrificing Your Son, Jesus. You beat sin and death and the devil. Help me to be faithful to You by spreading the Good News of Jesus and salvation by grace through faith. In His name I pray. Amen.

Questions to consider:

1. Notice the way that Joshua reminds the people of God's faithfulness to them. How has God been faithful to you?

2. This isn't the first time that Joshua has gathered the people for a renewal of the covenant. Read Joshua 8:30-35. What similarities and differences do you see between Joshua 24 and Joshua 8?

3. Complete this exercise patterned after the covenant renewal in Joshua 24:
   - Name one thing God has done for you or your family (vv. 2-13).
   - List one specific commitment to God you want to make (vv. 14-18).
   - Write on paper the "god" you wish to forsake (vv. 23-24).
   - Crumple your paper and throw it in the wastebasket (or fire).
   - Celebrate your forgiveness and God's faithfulness with prayer or a song of praise.

Week 18: My Shepherd

Read Psalm 23 – A Psalm of David

"The Lord is my shepherd…"

King David penned those words, but have you ever really thought about what they mean? We say them at funerals, but they are not about death. Instead, they are an invitation to life. We see them portrayed in still pictures with no movement, but this Psalm is dynamic and alive. We think of them as describing the past, yet they are relevant every moment of every day—24/7. Few of us have ever been a shepherd or been around sheep, but these words are about God and His people. David, who was a shepherd, understood that these are the words of unceasing care, of relentless attention, of constant protection, and of extreme grace.

Jesus said, *"I am the good shepherd; I know my sheep and my sheep know me…"* (John 10:14). Upon hearing her pastor speak the words of Psalm 23, a woman stated that this was the best reading of these words she had ever heard…better than any actor or Biblical professor. Why? Because she knew the reader knew the Shepherd. There was relationship. Do the words of Psalm 23 reflect a relationship between you and the Good Shepherd? Do they give you confidence and comfort? Do they describe your life? Or do you live worried and weighed down by the burdens and busyness of life? Making a way through our todays and tomorrows can cause us to miss our Good Shepherd and the benefits that He brings.

The Lord is <u>my</u> Shepherd. God's relationship with me is personal. He leads me to green pastures and quiet waters. He gives me good times and the joy that they bring. He offers peace when I am upset and anxious.

He restores my soul when I feel far from Him. He refreshes my spirit when I am exhausted by the conflicts and obstacles of life.

He keeps me on the right path, the path that leads to Him, the path of forgiveness and salvation. Sometimes I walk through some dangerous and deadly places, and I try to do it by myself, without God. Still, I don't have to be afraid. He is bigger than all of my struggles. He loves me no matter what.

He has defeated all of my enemies. I am not defined by my losses but His victory. I can soar with new possibilities and hope. I can live out my unique giftedness because He fills me up.

Goodness and love follow me around like a light cloud over my head. He will be a friend who will never leave me. And because of my Shepherd and His sacrifice on the cross, because of the empty tomb, because of the faith that He gives me, I will dwell in His house, the place He prepares for me, forever.

Pause and drink in these words. Commit them to memory and live envisioning your Shepherd with you always, watching you always, saving you always, empowering you always. With all that our Good Shepherd offers, we shall not want. What a way to live! All thanks to "my Shepherd."

My Shepherd, You have been so good to me. You give me blessings for here and hereafter. Thank You. Help me to not lose sight of You. Keep me tuned in to Your voice. You know me...keep me knowing You forever and ever. Amen.

An exercise or two to grow you:

- Try to paraphrase and personalize this psalm. Put it in your own words.

- Journal for a week or longer about the way that the Lord is your Shepherd.

Week 19: Am I Really Loved?

Read 1 Samuel 16 – The Anointing of King David

There is an old story of Adam saying to Eve, "Do you love me?" "Yes," Eve responds. "No, do you really love me?" insists Adam. "Of course," she reassures. "Really, truly? You love me?" he asks once more. Eve looks around and throws her hands up saying, "Adam, who else?"

Something within all of us wonders whether we are good enough, whether we measure up, whether we are loved. We have a sense of insecurity. Our world constantly suggests Mom and Dad love our siblings more. Our coworkers are more successful than we are. We are not as bright or athletic or musical as our friends. We do not have as much or are not as significant as our neighbors.

Pay attention to advertising, and there is always that subtle message that we are not good enough the way we are. If only we would purchase the product being advertised, then we might be more loveable. So, we buy whatever is being sold only to discover time and again that being loved involves something more.

David lived nearly a thousand years before the time of Christ. He was the youngest of eight sons born to Jesse, his father. As a boy and into his teen years, David's job was to care for sheep. When David was growing up, Saul was the king of Israel. But King Saul was disobedient to God and displeased Him so much that God decided to remove him from his leadership of the Israelites. God then directed Samuel, the prophet and spiritual leader of the time, to anoint a new king. God sent him to Bethlehem, to the house of Jesse, because God said one of Jesse's sons would be the next king. Jesse gathered all of his family and almost all of his sons to meet Samuel.

Samuel was anxious to choose the next king, but he considered height and strength and attractiveness and intelligence and leadership ability as the keys to selecting the next king. David was too young, too average, too nondescript—certainly not king material. In verse 7, God speaks to Samuel, *"Do not consider his appearance or his height...The LORD does not look at the things man looks at. Man looks at outward appearance, but the LORD looks at the heart."* While David was young, average, and smaller than the others, his heart was large toward God. And so it was that God said to Samuel, "He's the one. Anoint him king."

How often and easily we use the typical measures and values of this world to evaluate ourselves and other people. We forget that God has an entirely different way of looking at us. We may judge ourselves and each other by our net worth, by what we do, our achievements or degrees or honors, the kind of house we live in, the car we drive, the job we have, the clothes we wear, or the grades we get. God just loves us, no matter what we have. He died on the cross for all people, good and bad. He gifts all people who come into His family and loves us all the same. As our eyes and hearts are focused on Him, we understand this amazing truth: *"How great is the love the Father has lavished on us, that we should be called children of God! And that is what we are!"* (1 John 3:1-2).

Lord God, thank You for loving me. Forgive me for the times when I feel inferior, as if You have not given me enough. Forgive me for the times when I have looked at my world through the lens of this world instead of through Your loving eyes. Help me always to remember that You sent Your Son to die for me. Can there be any greater love than that? Help me also to live the victory that He won over my sense of not measuring up. In His powerful and loving name I pray. Amen.

An exercise for growth:

1. In what ways do you feel inadequate? Inferior? What are some causes for these feelings?

2. Read some verses from the Bible about God's great love for you: Matthew 10:29-31, Jeremiah 1:4-5, Psalm 139:15-16, Jeremiah 2:11, and Romans 8:35-39.

3. Continue your search for verses and make a list in your Bible. Memorize one or more of these verses and recite them daily, especially when you feel inadequate or inferior.

Week 20: Revival
Read 2 Chronicles 7 – The Dedication of the Temple

In a sermon, David DeWitt[9] tells of a young ministerial student named Evan Roberts, who in 1904 began to feel that God was sending him to proclaim a message of revival in Wales, which is now a part of Great Britain. Roberts asked his home church to preach this message of revival, but his pastor was reluctant to allow him to speak. In a compromise, the pastor announced that Roberts would be speaking following the regular prayer meeting, and any who wished to stay were welcome. Only 17 people stayed to hear Evan speak, and most of them were teenagers and young adults.

Evan Roberts spoke in that church for nearly two hours with a simple four-point message that he was convinced God would use to bring revival:
1. Confess all known sin to God.
2. Deal with and get rid of any sinful area of your life.
3. Be ready to obey the Holy Spirit instantly.
4. Confess Christ publicly.

When Roberts was finished speaking, all 17 young people were at the altar on their knees crying out to God. They prayed until 2:00 AM that night. It was the beginning of one of the greatest evangelistic movements of God in history. By the end of the week, over 60 people came to believe in Christ and, over the course of the next year and a half, revival swept through the nation of Wales. Over 1 million people were led to receive saving faith in Jesus Christ.

The revival was so great that the national culture changed dramatically. A rage of bankruptcies took place because all of the taverns and liquor stores went out of business. Work at the coal mines was brought to a near standstill because the mules that pulled the wagons were so accustomed to hearing foul language from the workers and, after the men were saved, the mules no longer recognized their voices or commands. The entire police force was dismissed for almost

---

[9] This devotion is from a sermon by David DeWitt preached September 19, 2005, published on sermoncentral.com.

18 months due to a complete lack of crime. The revival eventually made its way across the Atlantic and swept through parts of New York and New Jersey. There was even a daily column in the New York Times called "Today's Converts" that listed those who were being saved.

Times seem to have totally changed, and we have to admit that our world is nothing like that of 1904. We sometimes think that our Christian way of life won't survive. We wonder some days whether our marriages and families will endure. We get frightened for the futures of our children. We watch values and morals reach seeming all-time lows. We see a lack of integrity among our leaders. Many people aren't even considering God or His ways anymore. Can we survive? Sometimes, it seems almost inconceivable to consider a revival today.

But has God changed from 1904 to today? Is God's love any smaller now than before? Did Jesus' sacrifice on the cross have an expiration date? What part of the power of Christ's resurrection has diminished from then until now? What part of the work of the Holy Spirit has changed?

2 Chronicles 7:14 states, "...if my people, who are called by my name, will humble themselves and pray and seek my face and turn from their wicked ways, then will I hear from heaven and will forgive their sin and will heal their land."

This chapter is about the dedication of the Temple built for the worship of God. Solomon had finished the plans of God first revealed to his father, David. He had constructed a majestic stationary replica of the Tabernacle. But this day was not about a building. It was about rededicating hearts to God. Solomon had to recommit his heart to God through confession and forgiveness. Like the 1904 revival, the people of God followed Solomon's lead. Now they were able to live the decrees and commands of the Triune God for whom this temple was built. As they committed themselves to Him, God would empower their survival as a nation and heal their individual marriages, families, and lives.

Martin Luther tells us that our baptisms are to be relived every day. Just as we were washed clean in the water connected to God's Word, every day we are to confess our failings to God and, in faith, receive the forgiveness that He won on the cross. Our confession and forgiveness are then accompanied by a recommitment of our lives to God's ways and truths. He has died and risen to empower this daily revival. This daily revival is our only hope to survive the challenges of each day and to thrive in our Christian living, relationships, decisions, and commitments.

Lord Jesus, thank You for Your death and resurrection that save me from sin and all of its destructive consequences. Help me to begin and end each day with a habit of confession that leads me to the cross where I am renewed in the forgiveness that You offer. Don't let me stop there. Help me day by day to live according to Your decrees and commands. Following You is what life is all about, and You are my only hope to survive and thrive. In Your powerful name I pray. Amen.

Questions to consider:

1. When, how, and where can you build a habit of confession and forgiveness (of revival) into your mornings? Evenings?

2. Solomon was so committed in this chapter. What happened to Solomon in his life? Do some research to learn about Solomon. Why did he go astray? What can you learn to apply to your living?

3. Exodus 40 was another of our Great Chapters that talked about the dedication of the Tabernacle. Review that chapter and compare it to 2 Chronicles 7.

Week 21: Translating the Language of the Bible

Read Acts 2 – Pentecost

I'll never forget a conversation that I had with a person who knew nothing about God. He had grown up in a family that did not go to church (even though his parents attended church when they were young) and did not talk about God. They were a hockey family—their life was organized around practicing and playing hockey, traveling to hockey games (all year), and talking about hockey. He did get a hockey scholarship to college but, at the age of 23, was now done with hockey and ready for the rest of his life and marriage to a woman in our congregation, which is how I got to know him and talk to him about life without God.

The conversation was unforgettable to me because when talking about a relationship with Jesus Christ, I had to speak a different language to him. He didn't understand concepts like sin (couldn't understand why it was such a big deal) or believing or life or heaven or hell, let alone words like redeem or sanctify or justification or salvation. He had heard about Jesus and some of these words but had no clue as to what they meant. He came to church one Sunday, and I remember thinking that he must think we are speaking a foreign language. Who would translate? How would he learn about Jesus and His love? How would this marriage make it?

Acts 2 is the account of Pentecost. Fifty days after the resurrection of Jesus, the Holy Spirit showed up. There were wind and tongues of fire and the disciples speaking in other tongues. What made this so amazing is that people who didn't speak their language at all understood what the disciples were saying as if there were no language barrier at all. These people who spoke foreign languages understood the truths of God (salvation and love and death and resurrection) as if they were spoken in their own language.

Many people report that when they go overseas to Europe, Africa, or the Far East, it is unnerving because they can't understand what anyone is saying. Similar experiences can cause us to reflect on the Tower of Babel in Genesis 11. There, the single, common language of the people was confused (resulting in many languages) so that they couldn't communicate and thus, build a tower to make a name for themselves instead of God. Confusion and lack of understanding resulted and drove the people apart.

In Acts 2, when the Holy Spirit came, the many languages became one as God undid all of the confusion and lack of understanding.

Isn't it interesting that the disciples really didn't get it about Jesus and His death and resurrection until *"...He opened their minds so they could understand the Scriptures"* (Luke 24:45)? The Holy Spirit specializes in opening minds to hear the truths of God in a language we can understand. This means that, before we speak God's Word to others in a witnessing situation, we need to be aware of the language that we use but, most of all, pray for the presence and power of the Holy Spirit. Before we teach our children about Jesus or answer a question about God's Word, we need to depend on the Holy Spirit for the right words and that our message will be understood. As we go to church, Bible study, or in our personal devotions, we need to pray that the Holy Spirit would help us to get it about God's love and grace and salvation.

I wish I could tell you that the hockey player got it. I'm still praying for the Holy Spirit to open his mind.

Lord God, thank You for the gift of understanding Your truths. Thank You for giving me the Holy Spirit to translate Your message of love and salvation in Jesus to others. Help me to call upon Your Spirit to grow me in my understanding of Your Word so that I can share You with others. In Jesus' name I pray. Amen.

Considering God's Word:

1. Read Genesis 11 and note that the undoing of languages and the speaking in different intelligible languages (Acts 2) were both acts of God. Whom do you need to witness to? Are you speaking their language? Are you taking too much responsibility on yourself to make them get it? Pray right now for the strength and dependence on the Holy Spirit that you need to witness the truths of Jesus.

2. Consider the way that the early Christians lived as described in verses 42-47. What changes need to happen in your life to realize this living in the Spirit of God?

Week 22: The Power of Yes!
Read Isaiah 6 – The Calling of Isaiah

"For much of my adult life I've been shackled by fear. I've been afraid to try new things, afraid to meet new people, afraid of doing anything that might lead to failure. This fear confined me to a narrow comfort zone," said an unknown volunteer.

Have you ever felt that way? The World Volunteer Web[10] suggests that we should all step out of our comfort zones and volunteer; say yes! According to their website (www.onlinevolunteering.org), there are so many benefits. Volunteering can help you to learn a new skill, be a part of your community, boost your career options, develop an interest or hobby, gain new experiences, or send a signal to your teacher or employer that you are a well-rounded person. There are so many benefits to saying yes.

When Isaiah said, "Here I am. Send me!", he and God had something very different in mind. Look closely at verses 9 and 10. It sounds like Isaiah is volunteering to speak to people who aren't going to pay attention, who will inevitably ignore his message. Look at verses 11-13. It sounds like Isaiah will have to do this until the people are defeated and destroyed and devastated. How would you like to volunteer for that kind of a hopeless mission?

But it really wasn't hopeless. The people of God had become so corrupt that they would not listen until they faced defeat and destruction. They would not pay attention to the Truth of God until they faced the judgment of God. Isaiah's task was to call them to repentance, even when they would not listen, so that when the time was right, some would listen and return to God.

These are some of the hardest tasks that God gives us. We are called to keep teaching our rebellious teen about Jesus, even though they won't listen until humbled by a difficult defeat. We are called to speak the truth to a friend about being faithful in his or her marriage, even though the best hope for them to really listen may only happen when

---

[10] The website is www.volunteerweb.org.

they are found out or their marriage is on the rocks. We are called to keep inviting family members or friends into a life-giving relationship with Jesus, even though they may ignore us and even despise our efforts until tragedy strikes and they suddenly ask us to tell them about the only hope of the world—Jesus. These are the tough tasks of being a follower of Christ.

During these missions, we can question ourselves. We might challenge God and wonder why we persist. We can get very frustrated. During these times, God reminds us that He loves us, that He is truth, and that we are His beloved children. He tells us that He is with us and for us and that He works miracles beyond what we can imagine.

There may be some blessings while on our mission. God may grow us in our faith. We might learn patience and empathy. The person to whom we are witnessing may be transformed quickly or miraculously, which causes us a great amount of joy. Regardless, we say yes because God calls us to go. We remember that the mission isn't about the benefits that we get from saying yes; it is about being faithful to God and His call.

Can you say, "Here I am. Send me!"?

Lord Jesus, You are my rock and salvation. You give me life, but sometimes to follow You is a great challenge. Help me to be faithful to Your call. Don't let me get tired of doing what You want me to do. Keep me praying for those in my life who don't know You and Your love. Keep me witnessing even when I feel ignored. In Your encouraging name I pray. Amen.

Questions to consider:

1. What do you need to say yes to God about? What are the challenges and obstacles that may cause you frustration? Are you prepared to go to God as you face them?

2. What verses encourage you to say yes to God?

3. What do 1 Peter 5:12-19 and James 5:7-8 teach you in the challenges you face to be faithful to God's calling?

Week 23: Substitute

Read Isaiah 53 – Suffering Servant

In his book, <u>Written in Blood</u>, Robert Coleman tells the story of a little boy whose sister needed a blood transfusion. The doctor explained that she had the same disease the boy had recovered from two years earlier. Her only chance for recovery was a transfusion from someone who had previously conquered the disease. Since the two children had the same rare blood type, the boy was the ideal donor.

"Would you give your blood to Mary?" the doctor asked. Johnny hesitated. His lower lip started to tremble. Then he smiled and said, "Sure, for my sister." Soon the two children were wheeled into the hospital room—Mary, pale and thin; Johnny, robust and healthy. Neither spoke, but when their eyes met, Johnny grinned.

As the nurse inserted the needle into his arm, Johnny's smile faded. He watched the blood flow through the tube. With the ordeal almost over, his voice, slightly shaky, broke the silence. "Doctor, when do I die?" Only then did the doctor realize why Johnny had hesitated, why his lip had trembled when he'd agreed to donate his blood. He thought giving his blood to his sister meant giving up his life. In that brief moment, he'd made his great decision to substitute his life to save his sister.[11]

Unmistakably, Isaiah 53 speaks of the Lord Jesus Christ. Every detail of the prophet's words corresponds closely to the person and work of Jesus.[12] Written over 700 years before Christ's sacrificial death, Isaiah's predictions are so specific that no mere human could possibly have written them—or fulfilled them. This chapter is proof that the God who makes history inspired the Bible. The words of Isaiah 53 affirm the divinity of Jesus Christ.

---

[11] Thomas Lindberg tells the story from the book, <u>Written in Blood</u>, by Robert Coleman.

[12] Significantly, the Jewish Targum interprets this portion of Isaiah's prophecy as referring to the Messiah. A Hebrew Targum is a written Aramaic translation of the Bible.

The clear teaching in this chapter is that deliverance for all people comes by the substitutionary suffering of the Servant—Jesus Christ. He suffered in our place. He suffered because we have sinned. We deserve death and hell, but Jesus would not let that happen. He went to the cross for us. Because He did, we do not need to experience the horrible, eternal consequences that we deserve. Now relationship with God is possible for us as we come to Him confessing our sinfulness and turn to follow Christ Jesus.

Notice the terms of suffering packed together in these verses: griefs, pains, stricken, smitten, afflicted, pierced, crushed, punished, and welts. Is it any wonder Jesus cried "No!" to this cup of suffering in the Garden of Gethsemane? Still, He took the cup of God's wrath. He bore our burdens. He received our punishment. He was crushed for our rebellion.

Also, notice the contrast between *He* and *our*. Isaiah reports that although *we* did not recognize it at first, the sufferings of the Servant were not *His* own fault, as *we* thought, but were in fact the result of *our* sins and resulted in *our* healing. The Servant is indeed characterized by griefs and sorrows, but they were not *His* own. It was all for us that *He* suffered and died! All who recognize that their sins have caused the Servant, Jesus Christ, to suffer may include themselves in the all-inclusive *we*.

The atoning death of Christ is a truth so profound that humankind has been unable to fully plumb its depths. Think of it—Jesus, God's Son, died to pay the penalty for our sins! Various theories have been advanced to explain what happened, but the Bible clearly teaches that substitution is the heart of this great mystery. Jesus, the Innocent Substitute, bore the sins of all humanity.

Lord Jesus Christ, Thank You! Thank You! Thank You! for being the Suffering Servant...for being my Suffering Servant. Amen.

Devotional exercises:

- Read this chapter every day this week.
- Spend 10-15 minutes contemplating the sacrifice Jesus made for you.
- Pray a prayer of thanksgiving each day.
- See if you can memorize this chapter.

Week 24: Certain in Uncertain Times

Read Daniel 7 – Son of Man

Daniel lived through some pretty uncertain times as an exile in Babylon. Life as he knew it growing up in Judah would never return. Everything was different under King Belshazzar's volatile reign. Death threats, idol worship, backbiting officials, puzzling dreams, and difficult problems were just a few of the things that Daniel had to face during his 70 years in a foreign land.

We're living through a time of challenging uncertainty: economically, politically, socially, and morally. Many have moved past the 2001 attacks on the World Trade Center. It seems a short time ago that words we had never before considered—Al-Qaeda, Bin Laden, and Taliban—were in the forefront of our minds. Twenty years later, we are concerned about pandemics, riots, social justice, and racial inequality. Our economy has been depressed. There are health care issues, international crises, and an overwhelming national debt. Mix that with aggressive divisiveness in our country, the breakdown of the family, and runaway materialism, and uncertainty has bred insecurity. Life will never return to what it once was for many Americans.

The great American hero, Benjamin Franklin, once said, "There is nothing certain but death and taxes." Old Ben had it right. You can count on very little these days. Much of life is unpredictable.

So, in this world of uncertainty, where will we turn for answers? Whom will we trust? What will we hold onto? What will anchor us in the storm?

In this great chapter, God gave Daniel a dream. The dream represented future hope for all generations. In the midst of great uncertainty in Babylon, God touched Daniel's heart and gave him a hope that he could count on. The first image that appeared was that of a churning sea (vv. 1-2). The sea is often used in the Bible to symbolically describe the troubled status of the world and serves as a backdrop for the hope that God gave Daniel. Notice the images that remind us of the certain things that we can count on with God— namely, that earthly kings and kingdoms will not survive, but God's

Kingdom will last forever. Evil will eventually be destroyed. Most of all, notice the clear picture of Jesus and the victory that He gives to us.

"Son of Man" was one of Jesus' favorite names or designations for Himself. When Jesus uses that term, He is stating that He is true man but also linking Himself to this vision of Daniel. Even more, He is stating that He is our only hope in uncertain times. God was saying to Daniel in this dream to be encouraged or lifted up because the Son of Man is coming. Jesus is on the way. Daniel was given the assurance that Hope is on the way in Christ. Daniel saw a picture of Jesus some 500 years before He came. What a powerful image!

If you and I would just capture a glimpse of Jesus like Daniel did, then we could face anything the world throws our way. Where might we find that glimpse, that vision of Jesus? In the Word of God, the Bible. John announced that Jesus is the Word who became flesh and dwelt among us (John 1:14). The Bible reveals God to us. It shows us Jesus.

One look at the Savior is all it takes. Jesus is a Savior we can count on. He's a person in whom we can trust. He's a God in whom we can have confidence. In your time of uncertainty, turn to Christ, capture a fresh glimpse of Him, and He will make all the difference.

Lord Jesus, in the turmoil and confusion of these times, help me to keep my eyes fixed on You. You are the Author and Perfector of my faith. You are the only One who can say, "It's going to be alright!" and actually mean it. You really bring peace when I face uncertainty in the world and insecurity in my heart. In Your powerful name I pray. Amen.

Questions to consider:

1. What helps you to keep your eyes on Jesus? Worship? Bible study? Other Christians? Make a list.

2. Read the story of the disciples in the storm in Matthew 14:22-32. What gave Peter the ability to walk on water in the midst of the storm (uncertainty)? Where did he need to keep his focus?

Week 25: A New Religion?

Read Jeremiah 31 – A New Covenant

Religion is either one of life's greatest blessings, or it is one of the sickest things we do.

Religion can be wonderful. Most members of a church would agree with that. Religion can be fulfilling, it can be instructive, and it can be inspiring. Religion has driven so much of human progress. Hospitals, schools, and communities have been built in the name of religion. It can be one of life's greatest blessings.

But could it be that religion, at its worst, can also be one of the sickest things we do? It can hurt. It can damage—even destroy. It deceives. It misleads. It can create judgment and tribalism. It deals in death rather than life. Think of some of the consequences because of a blind adherence to religion: prejudice, destruction of property, ostracizing, dehumanizing, suicide bombers, and terrorists. Remember the Heaven's Gate group in 1997? How could 39 otherwise intelligent, well-educated, privileged people decide to shroud themselves in purple and eat poison pudding on the basis of some notion of a UFO hiding behind the Hale-Bopp comet? Utterly astounding! We say that they must have been sick, but is it possible that the sickness was their religion? Remember, religion is either one of life's greatest blessings, or it is one of the sickest things we do.

Jeremiah stood outside the gate of a grand temple in Jerusalem some 2,600 years ago. He spoke of the sickness of religion. To the people of Judah who were arriving to do their religious thing, this troublesome prophet of God spoke very offensive words. Imagine—a guy who calls himself God's preacher having the audacity to stand right in the Temple gate and challenge respectable people, telling them that what they are doing is hollow and broken. Did they want to hear him? Do we want to hear him?

Jeremiah told them that God is making a new covenant that is not about laws written on stone. It is not about traditions and blind obedience to the trappings of religion. God is going to write His law on people's hearts. His Kingdom is going to be about a relationship with Jesus, the Christ. It will be about grace and love.

When we speak of religion at its worst, it is the sickest thing we **do**. It is a list of rules or rituals to be accomplished. It is information to know or perform. It is simply a to-do list that, when accomplished, holds out the fraudulent goal of making us good or fixing our lives. Religion at its worst is simply standards and advice to determine who is in and who is out.

Religion that is one of life's great blessings is something <u>God</u> gives us. He does something for us. He lived the perfect life. He obeyed all the rules and rituals. He accomplished the to-do list for salvation. He is the information to know as He reveals who God is and what's important to Him. True religion as a great blessing is about being loved and saved and then responding to what Jesus has done for us.

I remember one year when our daughter was very small, less than a year old. We were looking forward to giving her really great Christmas presents. But, at that young age, she was more interested in the brightly colored paper and ribbons than the toy inside. Sometimes, we can get more interested in the wrappings of religion than in what it is really all about. We get more caught up in the trappings of church and "doing church" than in the Lord of the church. To offer another metaphor: it's like giving someone a nice juicy piece of fruit, and they eat the peel and throw away the fruit—the best part.

You see, the real issue is not religion. The real issue is knowing Jesus Christ and Him crucified and where we stand with Him. Thanks be to God who wants to heal the sickness of the human heart, even the sickness of religion. Thanks be to God who in Christ Jesus has come as the Word made flesh to show us health and wholeness, life and love. He fixes our lives. Thanks be to God who in Christ Jesus is able to write His law on our hearts and make us good so that He is real. He is ours. He is personal. Thanks be to God who instead of a system gives us a person, His Son, Jesus Christ, whom we may know for ourselves.

Is your life about religion or relationship with Jesus? Is it lived in thankfulness to God for His inexhaustible gift? Is it "churchianity" or

Christianity? Do you really know Jesus Christ who heals all your diseases, who redeems your life from destruction, who crowns you with loving kindness and tender mercies? Do you know the One who is even able to heal the hearts of those infected with the sickness of religion?

Lord God, forgive me and forget my sins of making You and Your Kingdom about superficial things. Don't let me get bogged down in the institution of religion. Help me to know You and Your only Son. Help me to know love. Help me to know care for the poor and hope for the lost. Help me to live the new covenant that You have established. In Jesus' name I pray. Amen.

Questions to consider:

1. What are some things that you cling to that are really about institution and tradition—the trappings of religion—and not Jesus? Do these things and ways of thinking keep you from living and promoting the Great Commission of Jesus?

2. Read John 4:21-26. How does this conversation help you to know God's heart about religion?

3. Take the time to read through the book of Joel. Notice the consistent theme that true religion is about a relationship with God that shows itself in actions of faithfulness, love, and generosity.

4. Read James 1:26-27. What does James say about true religion, and how does this relate to Jesus?

Week 26: God with Skin On

Read John 1 – The Word Made Flesh

In the movie *Moneyball*, Brad Pitt plays the role of Billy Beane who was the general manager of the Oakland Athletics baseball team. What would that be like to see your life portrayed by an actor like Brad Pitt? When asked that question, Billy Beane used words like *surreal* and *incredibly humbling*. Of course, one can never really completely or accurately depict the life of another...unless that person is Jesus Christ.

John 1:14 states that the Word (God) became flesh and lived among us. We have seen His glory. In Jesus, we have seen God's heart. We have seen what God is like. We see God's love for people that prompts Him to leave the splendor of heaven and live on this sin-filled earth. We experience God in a way that we can understand—as a human being. He reminds us that He wants to make Himself known to us. He wants us to understand Him. He wants to connect with us. He shows us His love and power to help us in physical and tangible ways. We see God's power over evil and all that evil does as He miraculously heals disease, overcomes storms, and beats death. He is Light that we can see in a dark world.

What makes all of this so amazing to us is that Jesus is not acting or playing some kind of a role. Jesus really is God. He is the second Person in the Trinity. He is fully God and fully human. We use the word *incarnate* to explain this mystery. He puts flesh on God. At Christmas time, we celebrate an amazing reality. The miracle lasted 33 years[13] until Jesus ascended into heaven.

Now, He asks us to carry on His presence. He wants us to be God with skin on.

---

[13] Biblical scholars point out that Jesus began His public ministry at the age of 30 (Luke 3:23). Based on Luke's more chronological Gospel of Jesus, which makes Jesus' public ministry three years in length, the age at Jesus' death would be 33 years old.

In telling about Judgment Day, Jesus says that His followers (us) give food to the hungry, clothes to the naked, and water to the thirsty. He talks about the way that we visit those in prison and care for the hurting. This is God's heart, and He is asking us to do as He does. Previously, Jesus tells us to be lights in the world. He is the Light of the world. We are to be like Him. We are to be Jesus incarnate. We are to be the living, breathing hands and feet and voice of Jesus.

When someone is anxious or afraid, we listen to them and speak God's Word of comfort and thus become the presence of Jesus. We help our neighbor during a rough time and become the presence of Jesus in their lives. We visit someone in the hospital or help a young person, and we are Jesus to the world. Whenever we touch lives with Jesus' love, we are Jesus incarnate.

This is not acting on our part. We are not playing a role. Jesus has loved us. Jesus has died and risen for us. We have been given the gift of faith in Jesus. Our lives in Jesus are a faith-relationship that we live each and every day as a reflection of the heart of God, the presence of God, and the love of God. We bring light so people may see the Light who is Jesus Christ.

Lord Jesus, thank You for showing me the heart of God. Thank You for Your love and the life I have through faith. Help me to live my life as a reflection of Your heart. In Your name I pray. Amen.

Thoughts to explore:

1. Look at the way John begins his Gospel. It is the same way that Genesis begins: "In the beginning..." What do you suppose John is communicating to us with this beginning for his Gospel?

2. Consider the metaphors that the Bible uses for the Word. Since Jesus is the Word who became flesh, what do these metaphors teach us about Jesus (Ephesians 6:17, John 17:17, and Hebrews 4:12)?

Week 27: The Knowing/Doing Gap

Read Matthew 5 – Beatitudes

There is a gap that causes frustration and dysfunction in families, marriages, schools, companies, and personal lives. It is called the "knowing/doing" gap. Author and pastor, John Ortberg,[14] goes on to explain that it is the difference between **knowing** there is a problem, **knowing** that it is important to fix the problem, maybe even **knowing how** to fix the problem, then following through and **doing** something about it. The **doing** failure can be a result of laziness, a lack of discipline, or a desire to take the path of least resistance.

This is the gap that Jesus confronts in the Sermon on the Mount recorded in Matthew 5. People would hear what God wanted them to do. They knew how important it was. For a variety of reasons, they just didn't do anything about it. God in the Bible calls this failure to do His will and live His ways sin. Sin keeps us from God and all of His great blessings here and hereafter, which is why Jesus provides the only solution to this gap.

"Up there" in heaven, the knowing/doing gap doesn't exist. Heaven is perfect so everybody knows the right thing to do and does it. They do what God does. It only makes sense then, that "up there" has to come "down here" to close and eliminate the knowing/doing gap. God has to leave heaven and come to earth as a human being to take care of this gap of sin. This is Jesus' primary teaching point in this Sermon on the Mount.

Jesus, God Incarnate, came to bring the Kingdom of Heaven (Matthew 4:17, 23). He says, *"Blessed are the poor in spirit, for theirs is the kingdom of heaven."* Jesus teaches us to pray in the Sermon on the Mount, "Thy kingdom come." He comes to bring "up there," where things are the way God wants them to be, where there is no knowing/doing gap, "down here." He lives knowing the ways of God

---

[14] John Ortberg writes in several books and sermons about the knowing/doing gap, including "The Me I Want to Be: Becoming God's Best Version of You", published by Zondervan: Copyright 2010.

(the right things) and doing the will of God. He lives the way we cannot live on our own.

We are frustrated because we want to do good but don't end up doing that. We end up doing what we don't want to do. Jesus knows our struggle, but that doesn't change His expectation of knowing and doing good. He says that unless our righteousness surpasses that of the Pharisees and the teachers of the law (men who rigidly and doggedly defined and sought to obey every Law of God), we won't be able to close the knowing/doing gap. We can't eliminate on our own the gap between knowing the right thing and doing it. Trying very hard, discipline, reading books, having mentors or coaches isn't going to fix our problem with this gap, with sin.

Jesus has to eliminate the gap. He comes into our lives and changes us so that we can be like Him—both knowing and doing the right thing, the good thing, the God thing. We need Jesus to change us from the inside out. We need Jesus to do something out of this world. We need Him to transform us. He does that by dying on the cross to take our sins away. He takes away all of our failures of knowing and doing. When we don't know the right thing or when we don't do the right thing, He forgives us. He takes our sins to the cross and removes them. Even more, He exchanges them with His righteousness and perfection. He knew He had to die for sin and He did it. There is no "knowing/doing" gap with Him. When He gives us the Holy Spirit, we are able to live in a faith-relationship with Him that gives us the power to do what He says. *I can do all things through Christ who gives me strength*" (Philippians 4).

Lord Jesus, thank You for taking care of my sin. Thank You for letting me be able to not only know You but also do what You say. You are my only hope. You are my Savior. Help me always to have the strength to do what You say. In Your powerful name I pray. Amen.

Thoughts to consider:

1. Read John 14:15 and verses 23-24 and notice how Jesus connects love to doing what He says. Pray that God will grow your love for Him.

2. Read about Paul's struggle to do what Jesus says in Romans 7:15-25. Can you relate? What is Paul's only hope?

Week 28: Out of the Darkness

Read John 3 – Jesus and Nicodemus

Nicodemus was a Pharisee, a member of the Jewish ruling Council also known as the Sanhedrin. This was the group that attacked Jesus and eventually brought trumped up charges against Him, voting for His death. But something Jesus said must have caught the heart of Nicodemus. The miracles of Jesus had certainly caught his attention. He had to know more about Jesus, who He was, and what He taught. He had to ask questions. He had to talk to Jesus, but how? If anyone saw Nicodemus meeting with Jesus, they would think that Nicodemus was one of Jesus' followers. He could lose his job, position on the ruling Council, and even his family. The meeting would have to be in secret. Nicodemus would have to go to Jesus at night, in the darkness.

When together with Jesus, Nicodemus was confronted with some mind-boggling truths. People have to be perfect to enter the Kingdom of God, but all people are sinners. Jesus said that we have to be *"born again of water and the Spirit"* in order to escape this cycle of *"flesh giving birth to flesh."* (Sinful people have sinful kids). No amount of our doing good will be enough. We need Jesus to be perfect for us. *"For God so loved the world that He gave His one and only Son, that whoever believes in Him shall not perish but have eternal life"* (John 3:16).

Nicodemus was having a hard time understanding all of this when Jesus added, *"Light has come into the world, but men loved darkness instead of light because their deeds were evil. Everyone who does evil hates the light and will not come into the light for fear that his deeds will be exposed. But whoever lives by the truth comes into the light..."* Interesting, light and truth go together. Darkness and lies are synonymous. Jesus was telling Nicodemus and us that we need to come out of the darkness to live in the Light. Jesus is the Light. We need to live in Jesus.

How often do we have our dark places, our hiding places? We hide a sinful habit from our spouse or parents or boss. We hide behind a lie about ourselves or attack another to make us look acceptable. We keep a sin of abuse or neglect or addiction or unfaithfulness out of the light so that we don't lose our family or friends or job. Before long, we get used to the dark and get confused about what living in the light really is. We move further from the Light. We forget what light is, about who the Light really is.

This is not a call to have everyone bear their dark secrets to the world. This is a call to bring those hidden sins before the Lord, have that conversation with Jesus that has been needed, and confess. Do we really believe Jesus when He spoke the words of John 3:16 and verse 17 (*"For God did not send his Son into the world to condemn the world, but to save the world through him."*)? God wants us to have new birth and forgiveness. He wants the chains of sin broken. He wants us to have eternal life—life in the Light.

Nicodemus most likely did not participate in the trial to condemn Jesus or the vote to kill Him. He became a follower of Jesus. He lived in the light. Many others have followed the path of Nicodemus and come out of the darkness. It's a daily habit and victory that God calls us to. Will you live relieved, renewed, and healed today?

Lord Jesus, I spend too much time in the darkness. I hide my sins from others but most of all from You. This has only brought struggle and guilt and shame to my life. This has strained my relationship with You and those I love. Help me to come out of the darkness to experience Your love and grace. Take my guilt away. Move me to seek the help of Christian caregivers where necessary. Help me to walk in You, the Light of the world. In Your precious and powerful name I pray. Amen.

Questions to pursue:

1. What does this passage teach us about Baptism? Are you "born again"?

2. Notice the reference to the Trinity in this chapter. What verses speak of the Father? The Son? The Holy Spirit? What is the role of each? You may want to consult a catechism.

3. Verse 17 makes a statement that would be good for us as Christians, who are often accused of being judgmental, to model. What is it? How does it affect the way that you view and interact with others?

Week 29: Lost

Read Luke 15 – Parables of Jesus

We have all kinds of names for them: dropouts, dead wood, inactives, uncommitted, delinquents...unfortunately, the names connote judgment and seem to push them further away. These are the men, women, and children who have, for whatever reason, left the Church. The Bible simply calls them lost.

There have been numerous studies about them. They are on our hearts and our minds. Three decades ago, Alan Harre,[15] in Close the Back Door, pointed out that we who attend churches have not done a very good job of building authentic community. If people don't feel connected, they will quickly (within a period of months) move away from the Body of Christ. Almost every study since then has reaffirmed the importance of people feeling that they are loved and belong when they attend a church.

Interestingly, though, other studies indicate that while Christians can be very loving, we can also be very mean. Many who have left the Church have been wounded and hurt—sometimes by accident, sometimes on purpose.

Another book, Essential Church?,[16] asks the question about how relevant the Church is to what's happening in real life. If the Church is not essential to the struggles, joys, burdens, relationships, and challenges of life—why go?

Whatever the case, hypocrisy is highlighted in most studies about people who leave the Church. Christians who profess Christ but don't live faithful, loving lives that reflect Him can be poison to the Church and kill the desire of many people to be connected to the Body of Christ.

---

[15] Close the Back Door: Ways to Create a Caring Congregational Fellowship by Alan F. Harre; Concordia Publishing House; 1984.
[16] Essential Church? Reclaiming a Generation of Dropouts by Thom S. Reiner and Sam S. Reiner III; B & H Books; 2008.

The Church has gotten pretty defensive about people wandering away. Most churches ignore the issue and pass it off as the responsibility of the one who is lost, suggesting that each person has a responsibility to stay connected to the Body of Christ. Some churches' doctrine states that those who wander away never really believed in the first place, so let them go. Still other churches become judgmental and have communications that threaten the fires of hell if a person doesn't return to the Church. Many churches simply take a self-exclusion posture, putting in place a policy that after a year of staying away, the person is just off the church roster, out of the church.

All of this discussion about people getting lost gets really concerning when we realize that people who move away from the Body of Christ can and do gradually move away from Christ Himself. That's what Jesus is speaking to in Luke 15. These people are called lost because they don't have a relationship with Him.

Notice how Jesus treats this "lost-ness." He tells three stories and, in each, there is deep concern for the one (thing) who is lost. There is effort to find the one (thing) that is lost. There is great rejoicing when the lost is found. In all of these stories, we get a sense of deep love for all—including the lost. In all three stories, we do not hear words of judgment or names that condemn. In all the stories, Jesus reveals the heart of God: a loving, caring heart that desires that all people would be saved and come to the knowledge of the truth. Yes, there is responsibility that we all have for our choices, even the choice to wander away and squander the inheritance. Yes, there is a call to repentance. But most of all, there is a loving God who hopes that as many as possible will be caught up in His love and grace, a God who wants to bless and forgive and save.

Lord Jesus, bless us with a heart of love for all people. Keep us praying for the lost, talking to them, caring for them, and building community with them. Forgive us for sins that we might have committed, known or unknown, which might have pushed people away. Keep us faithful to You and rejoicing with all of heaven over one sinner who repents. In Jesus' name. Amen.

Questions to ponder:

1. Spend some time trying to empathize with the various characters in the Parable of the Prodigal Son. What is the younger son experiencing? Have you ever been in his place? What is the older son feeling? Does the older son reflect the committed Christian? Ever felt the same? What about the father?

2. Now put some names and faces to the characters. God is obviously the father. Which person are you? What does all of this mean for you right now? A character adjustment? Repentance? Love? Action?

Week 30: When God Waits

Read John 11 – Jesus Raises Lazarus from the Dead

As a pastor, I have often listened to the questions of those who are undergoing suffering and pain. Many of those questions ask why God doesn't help, why He doesn't answer, why He seems to abandon us at what seem like the most critical of times, why He remains disturbingly quiet. I have to admit that I have stopped trying to answer those questions. It is my role to be there and listen. It is God who has the answers, and we struggle to understand them and Him.

John 11 is an account that feels confusing at the beginning but in the end hopeful. It does not fully resolve the question of "Where is God in our pain?" But it may help.

Verse 5 reads, *"Jesus loved Martha and her sister and Lazarus. Yet when He heard that Lazarus was sick, He stayed where He was two more days."* Now granted, Jesus had just previously stated that the illness of Lazarus would not end in death. He stated that this was all about God's glory being revealed. But Mary and Martha, friends of Jesus, are in pain. They are worried sick. They watch Lazarus get weaker and weaker and drift away into death, and Jesus seems to let that happen—on purpose. This makes us wonder: was the first statement that Martha and then Mary made to Jesus when He showed up at the funeral (*"Lord, if you had been here, my brother would not have died..."*) one of faith or frustration?

What was Jesus doing? Certainly, we see His love, compassion, even pain as He comforts and weeps. Certainly, we see His power and glory as He raises Lazarus from the dead. Most of all, we hear the prevailing promise of the living God. *"I am the resurrection and the life. He who believes in me will live, even though he dies; and whoever lives and believes in me will never die."*

People have read this account of God's power over death for some 2,000 years and been comforted. Mary and Martha had to suffer for a couple of days for that to happen. Would you do the same? Suffer so that millions would be comforted?

Even more, through this account the conspiracy against Jesus was accelerated, which prompted His own death and resurrection so that all people might have the opportunity to live. If this waiting in pain for a few days would in any way advance the salvation of the world, was it worth it? Would you endure some pain for the salvation of a soul?

The Bible clearly indicates that God is much more interested in our salvation than in our comfort. He is Life, and that means forever. He wants us to live for Him and, one day in heaven, there will be eternal comfort. But now, on this earth, there is still a victory to be claimed. Could that have something to do with why we wait?

Does this help? The Bible is clear that God loves us. He died to save us. He is risen and therefore conquers sin and death and all of the pain and suffering that go with them. He showed up in the story of Lazarus and, when He did, the forces of evil and death were no match. He shows up for His people here to ensure our hereafter. We don't have to wait for any of these victorious realities. They are ours right now and forever.

Lord Jesus, help me to trust You when I am hurting. Remind me that I am Yours and that, in You, victory is mine. In Your powerful name I pray. Amen.

Questions to ponder:

1. Why do you think Jesus didn't go immediately to help Lazarus?

2. Can you relate to how Mary and Martha might have felt?

3. What strikes you the most about what Jesus said or did when He showed up?

Week 31: It All Goes Back in the Box

Read Matthew 24 - Olivet Discourse

As we approached the 2020 election with divisiveness, hate, protesting, and rioting, many Christians were wondering whether we were coming to the end times. Remember Y2K? The world was supposed to end at the stroke of midnight on December 31, 1999. More recently, the study of Mayan culture and the release of a blockbuster movie prompted many to believe that December 2012 was going to be the end of it all. I remember a book and several mailings that warned the end would come on a day that we had scheduled a church picnic. We never gave it a second thought, never thought of canceling the picnic and gathering in the church for prayer; we went right on with business as usual. When do you think the end will come?

Do you ever wish that you could have lived with Jesus and asked some questions? Often it seems that our questions never get asked or answered, but the question about the end of the world does. "Tell us," Jesus' disciples said, "when is the world going to end and how will we know?" Great question. We are on the edge of our seats waiting for the answer from the Son of God, Creator of the heavens and the earth.

In our day, we might place more value on what the book of Revelation has to say about the end times. Some have spent a lifetime trying to interpret the numerology, angelology, symbolism, and themes of this last book of the Bible. Let's listen to Jesus' clear words from Matthew.

Jesus first says that there will be signs that the end is approaching. There will be deceivers who say, "I am the Savior of the world." There will be wars and rumors of war, famines, earthquakes, persecution of Christians, many Christians falling away from God, increased wickedness and selfishness. These signs of the end are happening and even escalating. More have died in wars in the last hundred years than all of human history combined. The same is true with famines, earthquakes, and persecution. We can definitely see an increase in selfishness, and many are falling from faith in Christ.

85

Notice the last sign of the end. It is very instructive. In verse 14, Jesus tells us that the Gospel of Jesus Christ will be preached throughout the world according to God's satisfaction, and then the end will come. That Gospel message that Jesus Christ, the Son of God, is the only Way to life here and hereafter is now available in every corner of the world.

Every sign of the end has been fulfilled, so when will it happen? *"No one knows that day or hour..."* It will come like a thief in the night—unannounced and unexpected. And then...it all goes back in the box.

Ever play the game *Monopoly* or *Life* or *Catan?* You spend the whole game building a portfolio or a life or an empire but, sooner or later, the game ends and it all goes back in the box. You strategized and plotted and competed and invested yourself in accumulating all game, but when the game is over you have nothing to show for your effort. It all goes back in the box.[17]

Sound familiar? That is the way it is with our lives here on earth. We spend so much time accumulating and investing and developing and building but, when the end comes, it all goes back in the box. We can take nothing from this world with us when the end comes, which is why it is so important to realize that the most important gift we have is the eternal gift of faith that God gives us.

When we believe in Him and live our lives in grateful response to what He has done for us in dying on the cross and rising again, we are not about the stuff of this earthly life so much as we are storing up treasures in heaven. We recognize that Jesus is Life. We seek to be connected to Him in faith. We look forward to a heavenly mansion specially prepared for us by Jesus Himself. We invest in helping others to know Jesus. We make a difference that will last forever.

When we play games, we have no problem at the end of the game putting everything back in the box. The money and houses and hotels and settlements and cities that we accumulated weren't real anyway.

---

[17] *It All Goes Back in the Box* is the title of a sermon, sermon series, and book by John Ortberg. The full title of the book is <u>When the Game is Over It All Goes Back in the Box</u>, Zondervan. 2007. I remember hearing the phrase used by my parents after winning a game of Monopoly.

Maybe that says something about the stuff that we think is so important here on this earth. It certainly says something about the importance of living for Jesus, serving Jesus, and witnessing for Jesus.

Lord Jesus, help me to realize that one day it all goes back in the box. Use that thought to help me keep my priorities in line, putting You first, loving others as You have loved me, especially as I approach the end of time. In Your powerful name I pray. Amen.

Questions to consider:

1. What feelings do you have when you hear talk about the inevitability of the end of the world?

2. How ready are you to put everything back in the box?

3. What can you do to store up treasures in heaven?

Week 32: Abiding

Read John 15 - Vine and Branches

Jesus, in His infinite wisdom, chose not to be born in Minnesota and its harsh winters but instead in a grape-growing area like Israel. During the night before hanging on the cross to die, He spends some time teaching about grape vines and life. In the process, He unravels the most important truths of life and the essence of who we are as people. We may not like all that He has to say, but it is truth if we really have ears to hear (if we really think about it).

Grapes grow on branches that are connected to vines, which have a life-providing root structure. In a similar way, people are branches that need to be connected to Jesus so that we can be fully alive here on this earth and hereafter in heaven. A branch can have the appearance of being alive, but if it is not connected to the vine, it is not really alive. People who are not connected to Jesus can look alive, but sooner or later they will show whether or not there is a vital connection to the Vine.

This connection is revealed by the fruit that we bear. We will bear fruit if connected. If not connected to the vine, there will be no fruit. So...

Jesus says that we need to stay connected to Him, the Vine. He says to make abiding in Jesus your top priority in life. Notice the huge two-letter word "if" in verses 5, 6, and 7. There is an implied condition for life. We can choose to be disconnected from Jesus.

Athletes who give themselves completely to a sport use the phrase 24/7. Twenty-four hours a day, seven days a week they watch their diet, conditioning, attitude, rest, and training. They eat, drink, and sleep their sport. It is with that same commitment that Jesus calls people to be connected to Him. He wants us to commit to Him: His will, His Word, His love, and His strength.

Extending the analogy, all branches are pruned or cut back. Jesus teaches that even healthy branches must be pruned. This is often painful for us. We think it unnecessary, but just as expert gardeners know that pruning produces the best grapes, God knows that pruning us produces great fruit. (See Galatians 5:22-23 for a list of the fruit of the Spirit.) Without realizing it, we may need the blind spots of bad habits, prejudice, dishonesty, selfishness, and insensitivity pruned from our lives.

Jesus reminds us that the test of abiding is the bearing of good fruit. We can get so many wrong words in our heads. We are bombarded with images that fill us with messages to put ourselves first, consume, and ignore. God's Word has to correct these wrong words and set us on the path of life. When we are not connected to Jesus, we will not have the sustenance and nutrition for the fruit of the Spirit to grow in our lives.

Finally, there is a warning. Jesus teaches that disconnected branches are thrown into the fire to be burned. This is not an attempt to scare us. Jesus is only speaking truth. After a storm, what do you do with all of the tree branches that are in your yard? What happens to the person who does not abide in Jesus? There is justice in this world and for eternity. The world makes no sense without that truth, and Jesus is not hesitant to talk about it.

Jesus says, *"Abide in me and I will abide in you..."* What beautiful wisdom and truth!

Lord Jesus, thank You for Your wisdom. You have filled me with hope and meaning. Help me to stay connected to You so that I can always know whose I am and what really matters. Keep me from filling up my living with activities that have nothing to do with bearing fruit. Help me to bear fruit, fruit that will last. In Your life-giving name I pray. Amen.

Questions to ponder:

1. What are you doing to make abiding in Jesus the priority of your life? What connection is there between you and Jesus as you work? Play? Eat? Laugh? Cry?

2. Have you ever wondered if the struggles you might be enduring right now are related to the pruning of God? What sins might God be cutting out of your life? What fruit might He be growing (Galatians 5:22-23)?

Week 33: Relationship

Read John 17 – High Priestly Prayer

There is a trend in our country toward living alone. One of the reasons for this tendency is that it is more painful to live with someone who hurts us than to live with loneliness. Another reason is that we have created a vast network of "pseudo-community" options like texting, tweeting, Instagram, and Facebook to distract us from the reality that we are alone or lonely. Add to that our technology (television, Internet, cell phones, etc.), and we discover that our culture is creating an illusion of relationship that leaves us feeling disconnected and alone. Social networking is hardly social.

In John 17:20-21, Jesus says, *"My prayer is not for them alone. I pray also for those who will believe in me through their message, that all of them may be one, Father, just as you are in me and I am in you. May they also be in us so that the world may believe that you have sent me."*

In his book, Why Jesus?,[18] Ravi Zacharias states, "We became less than what we were meant to be." That statement reflects the heart of Jesus as He holds high the value of relationship or oneness. God is Triune. He is three persons wrapped up in one God. The Father relates to the Son (Jesus) and the Spirit. The Son (Jesus) relates to the Father and the Spirit. The Spirit relates to the Father and the Son (Jesus). He is, therefore, by His very nature relational. He created us for relationship with Him and with others. He wants us to be "one" as God is one. He prays that this will happen. He even says that the way people will know that He is for real is by the way His people have loving relationship with Him and with each other. Without a doubt, relationship is a big deal to God.

Since sin came into the world, this tendency we have for deep, meaningful relationship has been lost. With sin came personal exaltation, blaming, lying, hiding, and ruling over. How often do you feel as though you don't fit in, don't measure up, or can't connect? So many people lament a feeling of being an alien—sometimes within

---

[18] Why Jesus? Rediscovering His Truth in an Age of Mass Marketed Spirituality, by Ravi Zacharias; originally published 2012.

their own home. What is it about us that makes it so hard for us to have real relationship? We want it. We need it.

Jesus turns the question to the positive. Instead of lamenting the way the world has become because of sin, He comes to change it. He comes to restore human relationship with God and make it possible for loving relationship with each other. He defeats sin and offers victory to us through faith. He empowers us to be what we were meant to be. With His presence in our lives, we claim new ways of thinking, new habits, new attitudes, and new priorities that build—not destroy—relationship.

We value relationship with God and others. We take time for talking and connecting, not letting our tasks, time, or traits define us. We reach out and offer ourselves to others instead of being self-absorbed. A simple smile or hello is our habit. We are aware of what our faces and body language are communicating, and we guard them so that we build connection with others. There is a contagious culture that develops when we are around because we belong to Jesus and are one with Him. We become what we were meant to be.

Lord Jesus, thank You for the relationship that I have with You. You are my Savior and Lord. You love me. I am Your precious child. Help me to be a builder of relationships. Help me to pray the prayer You prayed that all of us may be one. In Jesus' name. Amen.

Verses to consider:

1. What do the following verses say about God's desire that we live in relationship? Genesis 2:18 and Genesis 2:24.

2. What do the following verses suggest can be a builder of relationship? Matthew 20:28, Luke 22:27, and Philippians 2:5-8.

3. What do the following verses say is the power of relationship? 2 Corinthians 5:16-18 and John 3:16-17.

Week 34: Who Me, Witness?

Read Matthew 28 – Great Commission

A young boy invited his friend to Sunday School. A woman listened to a young mother pour out her heart about the struggles of parenting her child through the terrible twos and threes. A golfer talked to his buddy as they played a round of golf about what was happening at his church. A teenager held the door open for an elderly person as he left the restaurant. A man played cards with a group of residents at the nursing home. A sixth grader came to the rescue of a second grader who was being bullied. A driver patiently let another car merge in front of her.

In which of these situations is someone witnessing? All of them. Every disciple of Jesus witnesses all the time in one way or another. The important question is: What kind of a witness am I?

Matthew begins this chapter with the resurrection of Jesus. This is the heart of the Gospel. Jesus didn't stay dead. He rose again defeating death, sin, and evil. There is no other event like the resurrection in the course of human history. The consequences of this amazing feat are realized by anyone and everyone who claims them through faith. Because of the empty tomb, we can experience joy, growth, relationship with God, freedom, hope, and living forever in heaven. Every human being needs these gifts, so at the end of this chapter Jesus gives Christians a purpose that can't be matched: *"In your going, make disciples of all nations..."* It is our privilege to share the gifts of Jesus' death and resurrection with others.

Following are some suggestions for being a witness of Jesus to others:
- *"Fan into flame the gift of God that is within you..."* (1 Timothy 1:6). As we grow in our own faith, our motivation for witnessing will grow.
- Pray every day for someone who does not know Jesus Christ as their Savior. Ask God to use you to reach that person.
- Build a relationship with a friend or relative. Do an unexpected act of kindness for this person for Christ's sake.
- Begin to talk about faith issues with a friend or relative.

- Support someone who is starting to walk with Jesus. Invite him or her to meet other Christians.
- Write a note or tell someone what Jesus Christ has done for you.

A summary of God's strategies for our witnessing would be captured in Jesus' call to love others. In a world that tends to question God's message and motives, people need to see the love of God—not just hear it. Jesus said, *"Let your light so shine before people that they may see your good works and glorify your Father in heaven"* (Matthew 5:16).

Lord Jesus, You have given me life and salvation. You rose from the dead. Move me to pay attention to others and to love them as You have loved them. Help me to be a witness as I go about my daily living. Give me Your words to say and the best time to say them. In Jesus' name I pray. Amen.

A lifelong practice:

- List at least three people in your life who don't have Jesus as their Savior.
- Begin right now to pray for them.
- Implement some of the above suggestions in witnessing to them.
- Find a prayer partner to support you.
- Find an accountability partner who will make sure that you don't forget witnessing—a privilege of living for Christ.

Week 35: The One for the Job

Read Acts 9 – Conversion of Saul

We live in a very specialized culture. If you want to practice medicine, you must attend medical school, complete an internship, and pass Boards. If you want to be a plumber, you have to serve an apprenticeship. If you want to be a teacher, you have to earn and maintain a teaching degree. Not just anybody can do anything. Human resource departments are careful to be sure that the qualified person is identified, researched, and hired.

Does God work the same way? Consider St. Paul. When we meet him, his name is Saul and he is overseeing the stoning of the disciple of Christ named Stephen. Acts 8:3 states, *"But Saul began to destroy the church. Going from house to house, he dragged off men and women and put them in prison."*

In his letter to the Philippians, Saul/Paul writes that he was eager and aggressive in persecuting the church of Jesus Christ. He tells us that in his dealings with people, he was legalistic—certainly not gracious or forgiving. This is hardly the resume of someone who we might want to be our friend or advisor. Congregation search teams would receive all kinds of red flags if such a person were to be considered as a pastor or teacher. We can understand how the apostles who spent three years with Jesus would question someone like Saul/Paul as a leader of the church and a church planter for Jesus Christ. What was God thinking?

Obviously, God's ways are not our ways. He loves all people and has the power to change the life of anyone, which teaches us some very important lessons. First, never give up on anyone. We all have people in our lives who struggle in their relationship with Jesus Christ or might not even have one. If God can convert Saul to Paul, a persecutor to a saint, He can convert our loved ones. Do you realize that if we give up on our loved ones we are, in a sense, giving up on God? Keep praying.

Second, we have to be careful not to judge. Sometimes, we are quick to see other people's faults. We wonder how they could be blessed by

God. We question how God could put them in a place or situation in which we think we are more deserving. In John 21:20-22, Jesus tells Peter to keep his eyes on his own life and not to worry about the perceived inequity Peter sees between himself and another disciple. "You follow me," says Jesus. Implied is the reminder that each of us is to serve and love as God decides. Great advice for us. God knows us best. He loves us and will use us during our lives as He sees fit.

Third, keep growing in Jesus Christ so that we can best be used by God for His Kingdom purposes. After Saul's miraculous conversion, he spent significant time preparing for ministry. (Read Galatians 2.) He learned about God's grace from the thorn in his flesh. He never stopped growing so that he would always be a servant for Jesus Christ. His humility and constant desire to know God and live in relationship with Him are a model for us as we serve.

Lord Jesus, thank You for calling me into Your family. Thank You for the privilege of serving that comes with being a part of Your family. Keep me focused on what You call me to do. Keep me passionate about growing in my faith. Never let me give up on my loved ones. Keep me praying for their eternal destiny no matter what their current standing with You. Your sacrifice and resurrection are life and salvation for the world. Be life for me. In Your living name I pray. Amen.

Learn more about St. Paul:

Pick up a book and read about the Apostle Paul.[19] Better yet, look up Paul in a Bible Concordance and read some of the verses in the Bible about him. The book of Acts has a great account of his missionary journeys.

---

[19] <u>Paul a Novel</u>, by Walt Wangerin Jr., Zondervan, copyright 2000, is an excellent depiction of the history of the early Christian Church and the role that Paul played in its beginnings.

Week 36: New and Improved

Read Ephesians 2 – New Life in Christ

When you see the words *New and Improved*, is there an immediate skepticism?

An advertisement for a toothpaste announced that it was *New and Improved*—guaranteed to give you whiter teeth and fresher breath. Do you know what was really new and improved about the toothpaste? The packaging. There was a new box with bright new colors and flashy print. The ingredients in the toothpaste were identical to the toothpaste's predecessor. It was the same old toothpaste.

Sometimes, we discover that what is new and improved is actually a repeat of something that was done before. Over the years, many foods have been advertised as *New and Improved*. The reality is that what's new is old; what's improved is something that dates back centuries, if not millennia. The food was not processed but whole with no preservatives added and no herbicides or pesticides used. In reality, *New and Improved* was the way it had been done in the past.

We can often get suspicious when a person who has struggled with an addiction or committed a crime *finds* God. We wonder whether they will act any differently or whether this will be some kind of new packaging that they will put around their behaviors. We wonder whether they will truly be *New and Improved*. The fact is, there are many people who question whether rehabilitation, transformation, or change for the good can happen.

In Ephesians 2, Paul describes the Christians in the church in Ephesus and us with words that we don't always acknowledge or appreciate. He says that we are dead in sin. He identifies us as followers of a selfish, evil world and the devil himself (ruler of the kingdom of the air). We need to be transformed and changed. In the words of Paul, we need to be "made alive." We need to become followers of God who is the only source of good and love in the universe. Through faith in Jesus Christ, God makes that happen in us. *"For it is by grace you have been saved, through faith—and this not from yourselves, it is the gift of God—not by works, so that no one can boast."*

Notice what being saved makes us. Alive! Not dead. We become people who are at peace with God and with each other. We are able to fulfill our purpose as God's workmanship doing the good He has uniquely planned for us. The Bible and its precious Word of God becomes our guide for thinking and doing. We are *"...no longer foreigners and aliens, but fellow citizens with God's people and members of God's household, built on the foundation of the apostles and prophets, with Christ Jesus Himself as the chief cornerstone."* This is more than new packaging. It genuinely is *New and Improved*.

Paul reminds us that we did not make this newness happen; Jesus did it for us. He died on the cross taking away our sin and replacing it with His righteousness. When we have a faith relationship with Jesus, He gives us that righteousness. He gives us that obedience to the Word. We are transformed in our thinking, focusing on Jesus. We are changed in our decisions, free to make healthy choices that benefit others before ourselves. We follow through with actions that reflect the loving heart of our Lord and Savior Jesus Christ. And when we fail, we go to the cross to receive forgiveness and strength to be realigned with Jesus Christ. Paul is correct in saying that Jesus makes us different from before. We are *New and Improved*.

Lord Jesus, thank You for the way You have turned my life around. I was dead; You have made me alive. I used to wander aimlessly; You have given me purpose. I used to think I had nothing but this world; You have given me supernatural perspective and the hope of a future in heaven. In You, I am *New and Improved*. Keep making me new through Your Word. I don't want to just know all the chapters in the Bible—I want to live them. The only way that will happen is by Your Gospel power and presence in my life. Give me Your grace. In Your powerful name I pray. Amen.

Digging deeper:

1. As you read the Bible, look for descriptions where Christ has made us *New and Improved*. Meditate on what each description means for you.

2. What are you doing to live the Great Chapters? Think in the areas of worshipping God, growing in your faith in Jesus Christ as your Savior, serving God by serving others, and being a witness of Jesus Christ to others.

3. Jesus warned often about being hypocrites (Matthew 6 and 23). He does not want us to be Christians in name only. He wants us to be people of integrity whose words and actions are aligned. Confess to God the times when your actions did not reflect your faith in Jesus. Let God forgive you and empower you to be *New and Improved* every single day.

Week 37: The Body of Christ

Read Ephesians 4 – Unity

"Later, Joseph of Arimathea asked Pilate for the body of Jesus...With Pilate's permission, he came and took the body away...Taking Jesus' body, the two of them (Joseph and Nicodemus) wrapped it, with spices, in strips of linen...At the place where Jesus was crucified, there was a garden, and in the garden a new tomb, in which no one had ever been laid...they laid Jesus there" (John 19:38-42).

Great love was taken as Jesus' followers took care of His body. They held it, cleaned it, prepared it for burial, and carefully laid it in a tomb. Three days later, God raised Jesus from the dead, and it was a *bodily* resurrection. Jesus ate food. Thomas touched Jesus. He had a resurrected body that then ascended into heaven.

Paul tells us that we as Christians are the Body of Christ. Jesus Christ is the Head of the Church. The church is His Body. Have you ever contemplated the significance of that statement: We are the Body of Christ?

Paul tells us that none of us by ourselves are this Body—we are the Body together. That means that each of us has been given different and unique gifts to touch the world with Jesus. We are Jesus with skin on to others.[20] We eat with others, building relationships with them. We touch lives with Jesus' love. We grow together, caring for each other and the world. This is an amazing opportunity and adventure, unmatched by anything else on this side of death.

Yet many people who believe in Jesus Christ don't realize that they are the Body of Christ. Gathering to worship is not on their minds or in their hearts. Growing to become more like Jesus so that they can reflect Him and enjoy His blessings is not a habit. Serving Christ by serving others is not what they think about. There is little awareness of giftedness to build the Body of Christ. Going to others in their school

---

[20] See Week 26 based on John 1, which describes Jesus as being God with skin on.

or neighborhood or workplace to tell them of what Jesus did for them is not a second thought.

There is an individualism that operates in our culture. Many say, "I don't have to go to church to be a Christian." "I can be a Christian and not read the Bible, know my spiritual gifts, or witness." And they are right. We don't have to go to church to be a Christian, but when you know Jesus Christ, you are a part of His Body, and He transforms you to want to worship, grow, serve, and witness.

Still others don't want to be a part of the Body of Christ. They see the institution of the church as needless rules and traditions. They view the church as being irrelevant and unnecessary, certainly limiting to the way they want to live. To be a part of an organization like the church is the last thing they want. Yet God always calls people into the Body of Christ. When we become Christians, we are baptized into the Body of Christ.

One of God's favorite words is ONE. The Triune God—Father, Son, and Spirit—is ONE. He creates marriage where two become ONE. He prays that His church would be ONE. He wants us to reach a *"...unity in the faith and in the knowledge of the Son of God"* (v. 13). *"From Him the whole body, joined and held together by every supporting ligament, grows and builds itself up in love, as each part does its work"* (v. 16). God doesn't want His Body to be broken and separated and disfigured. He is ONE and He wants His Body—Christians—to be one as well.

How do you see yourself? Do you understand that you are a part of the Body of Christ? Are you working, by the power of Jesus Christ, to bring your unique, God-given giftedness to the Body of Christ so that it can be what God has saved it to be? Are you growing so that the Body of Christ will grow? Jesus' body was broken on the cross so that His Body of believers would not be broken. May the power of the resurrection help you to see the power that we have together in Christ to be the Body of Christ.

Lord Jesus, help me to realize the great blessing of being a part of Your Body. Keep me from complaining about what Your Body should be. Instead, empower me to use my gifts to make a positive impact on others through Your church. Jesus, You died so that I might have this opportunity. Help me to live my life helping the Body of Christ to be one as You are One with the Father and the Spirit. In Jesus' name. Amen.

Learn more about the Body of Christ:

1. Read 1 Corinthians 12 and 13.

2. Take a Spiritual Gifts inventory[21] to determine your spiritual gifts. Then use them.

3. Note the fruit of the Spirit in Galatians 5:22-26. How do these help the Body of Christ to be ONE?

---

[21] Many Spiritual Gifts inventories are available online or through Christian congregations. It might be helpful to align the inventory you take with the ministry of your home congregation.

Week 38: Our Greatest Battle

Read Ephesians 6 – Spiritual Warfare

I am currently fighting the battle of Yorktown. The cannonballs are flying around me. Smoke clouds my vision and stings my eyes. The smell of muskets and gunpowder is thick in the air. Moans and groans of wounded soldiers create a dissonant disturbing anguish in my heart, but I ignore it. With bayonet exposed, I'm too busy fighting next to my white-clad friends from France who are helping me and others route the hated red coats.

As you have surmised, the war is not real. I am reading a biography of George Washington and his exploits as the Commander in Chief during the Revolutionary War. I can't imagine what some of our nation's forefathers went through as they secured the freedoms that we now enjoy. War was ugly back in the 1700s.

When I was compiling a family history, I spoke to my Great-Uncle Henry who served in WWI. He told me about the trench warfare that he experienced. I was a sophomore in high school, so this war seemed more like a fairy tale to me. Then I saw a story on the History Channel about the war. Can you imagine living, day after day, in muddy holes with the threat of poisonous gas and barbed wire all around you? Most of all—an enemy who was ready to shoot anything that moved. War was ugly then too.

Paul talks in Ephesians 6 about our greatest war: *"Put on the full armor of God so that you can take your stand against the devil's schemes. For our struggle is not against flesh and blood, but against the rulers, against the authorities, against the powers of this dark world, and against the spiritual forces of evil in the heavenly realms"* (vv. 11 and 12). This is our greatest war because it isn't against people (flesh and blood) who can hurt and kill us in this world but against the devil who can steal our soul forever. This is the greatest battle because it is against the rulers and authorities and forces of evil who instigate all the wars that history knows.

Note that this battle can often be fought in our minds and thoughts. The devil tempts us, and we think about what he wants us to do. The promise (which is really empty) is enticing. It looks fun. It becomes the focus of our thoughts. The temptation craves an outlet. It wants legs—action. So, the evil in our heart causes us to say evil, do evil, endorse evil, passively watch evil, or encourage evil.

We fight this war on a daily, hourly, sometimes minute-by-minute basis. The devil (which translates *adversary*) does not want us to realize the heavenly home for which we are saved. He wants us to think that we are either worthless so God won't help us or so worthy that we don't need God to help us. He is constantly deceiving and lying. He is subtle. One of his best strategies is to get people to think he doesn't even exist so that many, unaware, put their guards down and become susceptible to his advances.

We have armor to stand against the devil's scheme to steal our souls forever: the belt of truth, who is Jesus—the Way, the Truth, and the Life; the breastplate of righteousness, which comes from Jesus who is our righteousness; feet ready to run with the good news of Jesus' death and resurrection; the shield of faith in Jesus, who won the victory over the devil when He rose from the dead; the helmet of salvation, which was won by Jesus as He took our sins away on the cross; and the sword of the Spirit, which is the Word of God. Notice the common theme. Our weaponry to fight this greatest of all battles is Jesus Christ. In Him, we have victory!

Lord Jesus, You tell me to pray in the midst of the greatest battle, so here I am. I have sometimes misjudged the effectiveness of the devil's schemes against me. Don't let him convince me that I am so worthless that You won't help me or so worthy that I don't need You. Give me the full armor so that I can stand against the evil one. You are my only Hope. In Your victorious name I pray. Amen.

Learn more about your armor:

1. For each piece of armor, find other words in the Bible that help you to know what the armor is and what it does. Look for the words: truth, righteousness, Gospel, faith, salvation, and Word of God.

2. Learn about the weaponry of the ancient world as it is described in Ephesians 6. What do you learn about fighting the devil's schemes?

Week 39: Free to Choose Slavery

Read Galatians 5 – Freedom in Christ

During the Revolutionary War, slaves were sometimes offered freedom if they would join the Continental Army (Americans) to fight the British. Doesn't sound like freedom, does it? They were free to join an army where they were told what to do and when to do it, an army where they would be shot if they deserted. Some slaves chose this option and fought in the war and died, while others survived the war and received their freedom.

All people are slaves. Whether we realize it or not, we are slaves to sin. Have you ever tried to stop doing the wrong thing? We can't. No human being with the exception of Jesus Christ has ever lived a perfect day on this earth, let alone a perfect life. Not one. The Bible speaks of sin as though it were a power in our lives that dictates, controls, and is a taskmaster. We are slaves to sin.

What's even worse about this slavery to sin is that it leads to death. *"The soul that sins must die"* (Ezekiel 18:20). *"The wages of sin is death"* (Romans 6:23). All humans sin, and all humans die. We can't miss the connection.

How do we escape this slavery?

Jesus. He comes and lives without sin. The people who were closest to Him, living with Him every day for three years, said He committed no sin. Peter stated that Jesus committed no sin and no deceit was found in His mouth (1 Peter 2:22). John said, *"In Him was no darkness at all."* (1 John 1:5). Even more, Jesus defeats the power of sin. He gives that victory to us. The taskmaster, the controller, does not have any more power over anyone who is linked to Jesus through faith.

I look forward to heaven for many reasons. I want to see Jesus' face to face. I want to see again the communion of saints, which includes my father, grandparents, and many others. I want to experience no pain, tears, or struggles. I also long to be free from sin. I don't want this taskmaster dictating to me anymore. I want to do the right thing at the right time for the right reason with the right motivation for the right

Person all the time. My faith is fully in Jesus who has defeated this taskmaster called sin so that I can have that freedom from sin in heaven and here on earth.

That's right. In Jesus we are set free from sin here on earth as well. In Him, we have the power to say no to sin. When we sin, we are forgiven as we repent and believe in Him. I am free from having to do anything to get that victory over sin. Jesus just gives it to me through faith.

My response to this freedom is literally to give it up for Jesus. I voluntarily count it as a privilege to do what He says, what He wants. Paul writes, "...do not use your freedom to indulge the sinful nature; rather serve one another in love" (v. 13). Paul often referred to himself as a servant of Jesus Christ. The Greek translates *a slave of Jesus Christ*. We voluntarily concede our free will to become what Jesus wants us to be because we know that He is the only way to experience love, joy, peace, patience, kindness, goodness, gentleness, faithfulness, and self-control (the Fruit of the Spirit listed in Galatians 5). He is the only Way to real, satisfying life.

The Bible is full of paradoxes that confuse us. This is another: we who are slaves to sin are set free to become (by His power) slaves to Jesus Christ. What a blessing!

Lord Jesus, sometimes I see the Christian life as a burden, a slavery that is not good or fun. Thanks for the freedom from sin that You have given me so that I see Christianity as a joyful opportunity to live for You. Help me more and more to find sin less and less appealing, to desire more and more what You want—to love You and love my neighbor as I love myself. In Your name I pray. Amen.

Searching the Scripture for the Fruit of the Spirit:

1. Read Galatians 5:22-25. List the Fruit of the Spirit. Think about the ways that Jesus exhibited each fruit. Give an example of that fruit in the life of Jesus.

2. What fruit do you especially find prevalent in your life? What fruit do you find absent? On a 1–10 rating scale, rate yourself with each fruit. Meditate on this and pray that God would grow you in the Fruit of the Spirit. In one month, revisit this rating and see if it has changed.

Week 40: It's Not What You Do but Who You Know

Read Romans 3 – Righteousness of God

Several churches in the Twin Cities have support groups for those who have lost jobs. These groups provide prayer, someone to talk to, and camaraderie with others who are unemployed. They also provide support in finding a new job. One of the very important parts of this search is networking. A valuable benefit of these support groups is the connection they provide between businesses with work available and those searching for employment. Often in finding a new job, what's important is who you know.

When my father worked for the airlines, we would sometimes fly first class. What a privilege this was: good (better) food, unlimited drinks, a warm towel before take-off and landing, and constant service. The only reason we flew first class was because my father would upgrade us when there were open seats. (This was before all of the upgrading protocol airlines follow today.) It wasn't what we paid; it was who we knew.

A friend told me of an experience meeting a well-known athlete. As long as my friend was with this athlete, my friend received all kinds of privileges. He would go to VIP sections in the stadium. He received the best seat at a restaurant. "I'm with him" was my friend's ticket to all kinds of benefits. We all understand and accept (at least a little) that this is the way the world works. It's not what you do; it's who you know!

Ask a person how to get to heaven and they will often respond, "I'm a pretty good person. I've done this or that...and I haven't killed anyone or done anything heinous." The response is about doing. Its focus is what I've done. Why is it that when it comes to the ultimate, most extraordinary VIP experience there is, we disregard the who-you-know reality? When it comes to heaven, we think that it's what we do—not who we know.

In Romans 3, Paul tells us that we are all sinners. We may have some good in our doing, but none of us is perfectly righteous. The Bible also tells us that the only people in heaven are people who are perfect, without sin. So how do we get in? It can't be by what we do. None of us can be perfect on our own. It has to be by Who we know.

The Person to know when it comes to eternal life and heaven is the only perfect Person that ever lived: Jesus. His death in our place was so that He would be our righteousness. He gives us faith to know Him and His grace. When we die and stand before the Great Judge of all humankind, we will be humbled to hear Jesus come beside us and say, "He's with me," or "She's with me." The only way to receive heaven is by Who we know: Jesus. Jesus is the One who is God. Jesus is the One who beat sin, death, and the devil. Jesus is the One to know.

Our response is to count it a privilege to learn to say, "I'm with Him!"

Lord Jesus, You are with me and for me! Thank You. Help me not to stray from You. Even more, help me to walk closer and closer to You every single day. In Jesus' name. Amen.

Knowing Jesus:

Often the Bible uses the word *know* to reflect a close relationship with a person or with God. What do the following verses teach us about knowing God?

- John 10

- Luke 13:22-30

- 1 John 2:1-14

- Matthew 7:21-23

Week 41: Dead to Sin!

Read Romans 6 – Alive in Christ

A long time ago, a pirate decided it was time to return home. He had spent many years lying, stealing, and cheating in a faraway land storing up a great chest of treasure for himself. The pirate held on tightly to that chest because he saw in it something of much more value than just jewels and gold; he saw in that chest the fulfillment of all his dreams, hopes, and aspirations. The treasure chest held his future, his key to the good life. Upon boarding the ship for the long journey home, a huge tropical storm blew up. The waves and wind beat against the vessel until it began to break into pieces and sink. The pirate and his treasure plunged into the cold sea. With his arms tightly wrapped around his treasure, he began to sink. He strained and struggled, "How can I save my life and get my treasure to the surface?" Slowly the pirate began to realize that life was not in the chest but on the surface and that holding on to the chest would cause him to die. Reluctantly, the pirate let go of that chest and began to swim upward toward the surface.[22]

Despite what our culture claims, this time between birth and death is not about our agendas, egos, and possessions. Jesus is Life, and we can only be alive in Him. Yet, like that pirate, we hold onto our treasure chest thinking all the while that what's inside will bring us life. We have a simple choice: hang on to the stuff of this world and die, or let it go and live for Jesus.

Have you ever asked yourself, "How do I grow in intimacy with God?" Unfortunately, most people only have half an answer to this question! They simply think that the answer is to read more Scripture, pray more, attend church more often, or engage in the Sacraments more. This is not wrong, just incomplete. So, what is the answer? Growing in intimacy with God occurs as we die to ourselves (let go of our treasure) so that we may begin to swim upward toward Christ who is Life.

---

[22] The story of the pirate is a sermon illustration repeated many times. Stacy Nelson, cofounder with her husband Josh of *Legacy Ministries*, an online Christian discipleship ministry, used it in a blog entitled *Pirate Treasure*.

Dying to ourselves means that we die to sin. Jesus said, *"I tell you the truth, unless a kernel of wheat falls to the ground and dies, it remains only a single seed, but if it dies, it produces many seeds. Those who love their life will lose it, while those who hate their life in this world will keep it for eternal life"* (John 12:23-25).

What sins do we need to die to? Certainly our original sin. We don't just commit sins; we are sinners. That's why we say, "I, a poor miserable sinner, confess..." We also die to those rather obvious sins of greed, vanity, selfishness, lying, or cheating. What can be most difficult to die to are the sins that wrap themselves around good things. Sometimes, our family, friends, work, or fun can move us away from God. Sin can distort the value of these good things. We have to die to making them the focus of our attention. Sometimes, we need to die to our desire to control other people and situations. Sometimes, we have to die to our appetites. Again, nothing is wrong with having a sense of control or an appetite, but when they, instead of Jesus, become our treasure, we need to let go and move toward Jesus.

He is always there for us to provide us real life, love, joy, and peace that will last forever. He is present in His Word. He is present in the Sacraments. Our confession time is important because it calls for us to admit our sin and seek His forgiveness, which empowers us to let go and live.

Lord Jesus, thank You for Life. Help me to always recognize that You are the Source of True Life. If I am hanging on to a treasure chest of sin and the stuff of this world, help me to let go, to die to this sin. Fill me with Your love, joy, and peace. In Jesus' name I pray. Amen.

Coming alive in Christ:

1. Spend some time listing the sins that are drowning you. Write them down. Confess them to God. Pray for God to fill you with Him and His blessings. Now look for ways to fill the space of the sin that you have let go of: acts of service, generosity, prayer, worship, growth, and witnessing.

2. Meditate on Romans 6:11-13.

Week 42: God and Gecko Feet

Read Romans 8 – God's Great Love for Us

What would God and gecko feet have in common? What a crazy thought! But think about it. For years, biologists have been amazed by the power of gecko feet. These five-ounce lizards produce an adhesive force roughly equivalent to carrying nine pounds up a smooth wall without slipping. If we had gecko feet, it would be the equivalent of a 150-pound person walking up a smooth wall with a 1,440-pound cow on their back. So strong is this adhesion that polymer scientists have invented Geckskin, a device that can hold 700 pounds on a smooth wall.

So, what does this have to do with God and Romans 8? Listen again to these words, *"Who shall separate us from the love of Christ? Shall trouble or hardship or persecution or famine or nakedness or danger or sword?"* (v. 35). God is love. He sticks to us like glue with even greater adhesion than gecko feet. We can't get His love off of us—nothing can!

Everybody experiences trouble in their lives. We have all sinned. Sin's characteristic tendency is to separate. It separates families, friendships, and marriages. It makes us feel as though we are separated from God. But no, He is still there, stuck to us.

Hardship is tough on us. To go through a financial loss or a relationship conflict or an illness can feel so heavy. Sometimes these hardships cause us to feel unnecessary guilt and shame that can only make the load heavier. We wonder what people will think of us. Some turn away. When we go through hardships, we often find out who our true friends really are. God is always with us. He is like glue. Nothing can separate us from Him and His love.

Sometimes we are attacked because we do the right thing. Because we are Christians, we are persecuted. It is so easy at such times to question God. We can cry out like the Psalmists, "Why me?" Some under such stress move away from God, but He does not move away from us. His love is sticky.

We can feel vulnerable and afraid in this threatening world, which can make us want to curl up in a ball and protect ourselves. As time goes on, we take fewer risks. We make it a priority to remain safe. Comfort becomes our god as we try to control our environment. All of this subtly moves us away from the true God and a faith relationship with Him. Still, God is not intimidated or threatened. He sticks with us. Nothing can push Him away.

The list of things that might separate us from God's love, given by St. Paul in Romans 8, culminates with death. Some think of death as the end of it all. Psychologists tell us that the greatest of all stressors is the loss of a loved one. In our grief, we go through stages of anger, depression, and bargaining. God seems to be nowhere near us, yet He is there. *"For I am convinced that neither death nor life, neither angels nor demons, neither the present nor the future, nor any powers, neither height nor depth, nor anything else in all creation, will be able to separate us from the love of God that is in Christ Jesus our Lord"* (vv. 38-39).

Lord Jesus, Your love for me is amazing. You are like a mother hen who gathers her chicks. You are a Lamb who lays down His life for me. You are sticky with Your love and presence, with greater adhesion than anything in all of creation. Thank You. Forgive me for my tendency to wander from You. May I reflect Your image by sticking close to those in my life who are facing struggles. In Your powerful name I pray. Amen.

Some exercises of love:

- Spend some time memorizing the portions of Romans 8 that give you comfort. When you internalize Scripture, it is always there with you, even in rough times.

- Gary Smalley in his book, "The Language of Love,"[23] speaks of word pictures that help us to grasp the fullness and intimacy of love. What words from Romans 8 help you to grasp the love that God has for you?

---

[23] The Language of Love, Gary Smalley & John Trent, Focus on the Family

Week 43: What in the World Do I Do?

Read Romans 12 – Living Sacrifices

How do Christians live in this world? How do we respond to television, social media, and the Internet? What do we think and do when confronted by the morals and values of the people around us? What is a Christ-like strategy for dealing with the politics of our time? How does a Christian respond to our culture? What does it mean to be "...in the world, but not of the world?" What does Romans 12 mean when it talks about not conforming to the patterns of this world?

About a half century ago, H. Richard Niebuhr attempted to answer these questions in his book, Christ and Culture.[24] He offered five possible responses that continue to be evaluated by experts. First, he said that some Christians have claimed that we should live as *Christ against Culture*. In this view, our allegiance is only to Christ, and a radical choice confronts every person: either to follow Christ or to follow the world. Since the Bible states that the prince of the world is the devil, this view sees the culture as evil. Christians should, therefore, condemn the culture and withdraw from it. This response has been practiced throughout history. In Jesus' day the Essenes isolated from culture, living as hermits. Some cloisters of monks did the same in the Middle Ages. Fifty years after Niebuhr's book, some are advocating this same reaction, criticizing, withdrawing, and isolating from the world—building a separate community away from the corrupt culture. But is this what Jesus did?

The second response is to live with the *Christ of Culture*. This Christ is the Christ who is a product of the culture to be embraced and understood according to the current intellectual philosophies and scientific thoughts that prevail in whatever era. This perspective would prompt Christians to blend into the culture, rejecting many Biblical morals and values. In the 2020s, some Christians are blending, perhaps even hiding from the world, to protect themselves from criticism. Jesus wants our light to shine for Him. Can we blend and show others Jesus Christ?

Publishing, 1988.

[24] Christ and Culture, H. Richard Niebuhr, Harper & Row, 1975.

The third point of view would be to see *Christ above Culture*. Niebuhr calls the people in this group "synthesists" because they want to bring together the values of Christ and the culture. Cultural expressions are basically good. However, they need to be improved and perfected by the Christian Church and those following the ideals taught by Christ, who is supreme over all. We all face the challenge of "synthesism." The Bible teaches that we are in the world, but not of the world. How can cultural values which align with the world, be allied with the values of Jesus Christ? Isn't Jesus Christ "...the way, the truth, and the life?" (John 14:6)

The fourth view is called *Christ and Culture in Paradox*. The paradox view says that both Christ and the culture claim our loyalty, and we live in a confusion or tension that is never resolved in this life. The culture may force us to do things against our conscience. Nevertheless, we have to live in the kingdom of God and the kingdom of this world. We just have to live with the conflicts it causes. This response creates some untenable situations for us as Christians. There will always be tension between the world and our Christian faith. We seek the victory of Christ and the wisdom of Christ as we journey through this constant struggle.

The fifth view is called *Christ the Transformer of Culture*. This view is optimistic about the ability of Christians to affect the culture. It believes that the culture cannot only be influenced—it can be converted. The result of the sin of Adam and Eve (the Fall) corrupted the good and perfect world God had created. The world and people in the world are broken because of this corruption. Christ Jesus transforms people. Christian people have and will always have a transforming influence on the culture. Jesus taught in his conversation with Nicodemus in John 3 that a new birth of the Spirit has to occur for there to be true transformation. Those who are transformed with this new birth look forward to a new heaven and a new earth, which infers an end to this worldly culture.

While these five responses are broad and may be difficult to understand, we might find help in parts of each Christ-in-culture view as they unpack what Jesus is saying in the Bible. We as Christians are transformed by the renewing of our minds, by the power of the Holy

Spirit, by the cross of Christ. We are called to be a community here on earth, which serves as a testimony and model of what God created and saved us to be. By our words and actions we, as Christians, are uniquely set apart from the non-Christian culture. We see the sin and sinners in our world but are not conformed to them and their ways. Instead, we tactfully engage the culture seeking to influence the people in it: serving, loving, and witnessing. We believe the Gospel of Jesus Christ has the power to transform people, hearts, attitudes, and minds. We see God at work, remain faithful to Him, and continue to touch lives with Jesus' love. We seek our God who has this amazing ability to transform people for Christ. We are Christ to the world.

What in the world do I do? Jesus Christ has saved me from sin and filled me with His love and righteousness so that I will be a disciple influencing others for Him even in a world that is hostile, scary, and broken by sin.

"Therefore, I urge you, beloved, in view of God's mercy, to offer your bodies as living sacrifices, holy and pleasing to God—this is your spiritual act of worship. Do not conform any longer to the pattern of this world, but be transformed by the renewing of your mind. Then you will be able to test and approve what God's will is—His good, pleasing, and perfect will." (vv. 1-2).

Lord Jesus, sometimes to live for You is challenging. Help me to make the sacrifice for You and Your ways. Sometimes to live for You is puzzling. Help me to see clearly that You are the Way. Sometimes this world is frustrating. Keep me praying for others, serving others, and witnessing to others. In Your name I pray. Amen.

Learning more about your SHAPE:

1. Pray that God would reveal more about your SHAPE: S - Spiritual gifts; H - Heart or passion in life; A - Abilities and talents; P - Personality type; and E - Experiences. As you discover your God-given SHAPE, you will be led into service in this culture.

2. Romans 12 talks about our spiritual gifts. Spiritual gifts are given by God to all Christians to build up the church. What are your gifts? Read Ephesians 4:11, 1 Corinthians 12:8-10, 1 Corinthians 12:28, and 1 Peter 4:9-10.

Week 44: What Happens When We Die?

Read 1 Corinthians 15 – Resurrection from the Dead

A funeral always begs the question, "What happens to us when we die?" It is interesting that many of the answers to this question come from people who have never died and returned to talk about it.

One of the what-happens-when-we-die ideas is extinction. When we die, like somebody blowing out a candle, our lives end. This notion believes we have no soul or spirit and is especially common among those who believe that there is no God. Since God did not create this universe or us, we are only here to pass on our DNA. Many people live this way thinking this world is all you get, so live it up. *"Let us eat and drink for tomorrow we die"* (v. 32).

Another idea that has been bouncing around for centuries is called reincarnation. We are simply life-forces connected to every other life-force in the universe. If we live a positive, helpful, influential life, we will be reincarnated to a higher life form. If we live in a negative, violent, destructive way, we will come back again as a lower form of life—a mosquito or something like it. If we are a human life-force, we could come back as a higher class of human: richer, smarter, or healthier. All of this can work well to keep people in their places here on earth, but in actuality this belief system is a hopeless, depressing struggle to escape the wheel of reincarnation that never seems to end.

A popular notion is that everybody gets to a heaven-like experience when they die. This is called universal salvation. There might be a few people who are so corrupt that they won't make it to heaven (who or what decides this is never really explained). In general, though, none of us needs to be too concerned about how we live here on earth because heaven's coming for us all.

Perhaps you noticed that each of these ideas removes the historical fact that Jesus Christ died on the cross and rose again from the dead. None of these ideas needs a resurrection or a savior, which would prompt St. Paul to start preaching 1 Corinthians 15.

There is only one person who has died and come back to tell us what happens when we die. He is Jesus Christ who rose from the dead. He says that everyone dies because of sin. After death, we are all judged by God based on whether or not we knew Jesus, whether or not we had a faith relationship with Him. He died to save everybody, but not everybody wants Him or His salvation. Those who have faith in Him, who wanted to live *with* Him on earth, receive heaven when we die. We go to heaven to live *with* Jesus. Those who chose to live *without* Jesus here on earth get to live *without* Him forever in hell. The primary characteristic of hell is that Jesus is not present there.

Whose answers do you want to believe about what happens when we die? Some people who are just trying to figure this death thing out or the One and only One who died and came back to talk about it? Jesus the Christ rose from the dead. He is the Savior of the World. He said, *"I am the Way and the Truth and the Life...I am the Resurrection and the Life. Whoever believes in Me will live even though he dies; and whoever lives and believes in Me will never die"* (John 14:6 and John 11:25-26).

Lord Jesus, thank You for saving me. I want to live with You here on earth. I want to live with You in heaven all by the power of the Holy Spirit. Amen.

Notes on 1 Corinthians 15:

1. Look at verses 3 and 4. It sounds like some pieces of the Apostles' Creed. Could this have been the first remnant of that creed?

2. How many eyewitnesses saw Jesus alive and could stand up in a court of law and testify that He had risen?

3. Read verses 35-49. Notice the kind of bodies we get in heaven.

4. Verses 50-57 are often read at the graves during the burial of Christians.

Week 45: Love Made Me Do It!

Read 1 Corinthians 13 – The Greatest of These Is Love

Why do we do what we do? Why do we commit so many hours in already busy schedules to help the hurting, teach children and students, and serve on committees that advance the mission of God's church? Why do we give thousands of hard-earned dollars to missionaries overseas, programs that feed the starving, and movements that seek peace and justice for the "least of these" in our society? Why do we tithe, giving ten percent and more of our income to help the Lord's Kingdom to come? Why do we do what we do? Are we crazy?

In a sermon, Pastor Bill Hybels suggests that there is a hierarchy of reasons why we do what we do. The first and perhaps lowest reason why we give is because of some sense of self-interest. We get something out of giving our time and our money. It may be a good feeling down deep or a pat on the back from our friends. It may also be that the cause that we support somehow benefits our family or may be connected to a loved one in our past. Whatever the case, it makes us feel good to do what we do. There is nothing wrong with giving for these reasons, but because there is a touch of self-interest, the reasons for giving aren't totally pure.

A second reason we do what we do is spiritual obedience. God has said in the Bible to give. He has said to give a percentage (such as a tithe or 10%). He has said to help the poor and look after the "least of these," so we do it. We obey. Again, there is nothing wrong with obedience. God wants us to be obedient, but there is a higher reason for giving, helping, and serving.

The third level or reason for doing what we do is spiritual thankfulness. God has been so good to us. He created us. He has blessed us with many good things. We live in one of the wealthiest countries and times in history. We are generous with our time and money because we are saying thank You to God. This is a great reason to give and many people give for this reason, but it is not the highest reason.

Fourth is a level of giving that is very significant: spiritual vision. Bill Bennett said, "I submit to you that the crisis of our time is spiritual. What afflicts us as a nation is a corruption of the heart and a turning away of the soul. Nothing has been more consequential in the unraveling of our society than large segments of the American society privately turning away from God. And to turn things around there must come a widespread spiritual renewal."[25] Many of us recognize the crisis of values that our culture is facing. We have a vision for a better future. We give of ourselves to make this world a better place, to be a part of this vision.

Which brings us to our highest reason for doing what we do for God—love. One day, Jesus was interrupted by a woman with terrible sins in her past. She wept at Jesus' feet, washed His feet with her tears, and then kissed them and poured perfume on them. Jesus said of her, *"Therefore, I tell you, her many sins have been forgiven—for she loved much"* (Luke 7:47). The passion and heartfelt affection that she had for Jesus drove her to spend money she didn't have on perfume to anoint the Savior of the world. She could do nothing other than to give; love made her do it.

This is the greatest motive there is: love. This is the love that Paul writes about in 1 Corinthians 13. This is the love that is *"...the greatest of these."* It is what prompted Jesus to go to a cross for us. It is the love that He has for us. It is the love that He gives to us so that we might be like Him.

Lord Jesus, I am a sinner in desperate need of You and Your forgiveness. Fill me with the deep heartfelt love that will motivate me to be a generous giver as You are a generous giver in giving Your life on the cross for me. In Your name I pray. Amen.

---

[25] The Book of Virtues, William J. Bennett, Simon & Schuster, 1996.

Looking deeper in Scripture:

1. Read the story of the sinful woman and her love for the Lord in Luke 7:36-50.

2. Read other stories of love and sacrifice: Luke 21:1-4 and Luke 23:26-49.

Week 46: Worship: What's the Big Deal?

Read Psalm 100 – A Psalm of Worship

The statistics are stunning. People are gathering for public worship less often. They go to church to worship fewer times a year. The younger generations are even less inclined to worship. Some of this may be a response to the coronavirus pandemic, which forced many churches to limit their onsite worship and move to live streaming worship. Granted, there are spikes in worship, such as during the holidays or when a calamity strikes. Still, the research overwhelmingly suggests that in the last few decades worship attendance at churches is dropping significantly. What's interesting is that comments from pastors lament the decline, even wondering whether worshipping weekly in church should be considered a Christian discipline anymore. So, what in the world is the reason for this shift away from worship?

Thom Rainer and Sam Rainer III in their book Essential Church?[26] point out that 70% of 18- to 22-year-olds drop out of church. They say that the primary reason is that church is no longer relevant, no longer essential. "It's boring." "I get nothing from going to church." "It doesn't apply to my life." "I'm too busy to go." "I'm too exhausted to go." These are common refrains that pastors and church leaders are hearing from even some of the most ardent of church members.

How different are the words of the Psalmist who writes in a way that suggests that all creation cannot help but worship God. It's almost as if there is an innate response that comes from any living creature, and that is to worship the Creator. Even more, this worship is anything but boring; it is joyful, filled with gladness and a celebration of the goodness of God.

The word "worship" comes from the old English word "worth-ship." It describes the worth or value that we give to someone or something. All creation is wired to understand that its existence is a gift from the Creator. That includes human beings.

---

[26] Essential Church? Reclaiming a Generation of Dropouts, Thom S. Rainer and Sam S. Rainer III, B & H Publishing Group, 2010.

God not only creates us, but He makes the creation for us. When sin threatened to destroy everything, He saved us. Worship is always Christ-centered because He is so loving. It really is not about me or my needs or my preferred style or my personal taste. It is an opportunity to connect with the living God who is life itself.

When we, the people of God, get fuzzy, distorted, or off track about worship, there are some significant results. We lose a sense of passion for Christ. Our faith is weakened, even confused about who God is and His great love for us in Jesus. Distance from God in worship leads to cold hearts, hard spirits, and even spiritual death. That is why we are warned not to get casual about our worship, not to have an all-about-me, consumer-oriented attitude toward worship, and not to get disconnected from God in our worship.

Someone once asked, "How could we survive without oxygen? In the same way, how could we survive without worship?" Make a joyful noise to the Lord!

Lord, thank You for being who You are. Thank You for the opportunity to talk to You and praise You and worship You. My spirit is lifted when I have spent time with You. My sins are forgiven when I hear Your words of forgiveness. My life is empowered when I connect with You in worship. Make my life a constant refrain of worship. In Jesus' name. Amen.

Four suggestions for worship:

1. Reflect on the Grace of God. Use John 3:16 or Ephesians 2:8-9.

2. Reflect on a part of God's character. Use Colossians 2:3 or 1 John 1:5 or other verses.

3. Use nature to lead you to worship God the Creator. Use Psalm 19 or other psalms.

4. Fill your day with worship breaks of confession, music, Bible reading, and devotional thoughts.

Week 47: Who Am I?

Read Psalm 8 – How Majestic Is Your Name

Scientists tell us that our sun is one of perhaps 500 billion stars in the Milky Way, the galaxy in which we live. They add that the Milky Way is a medium-sized galaxy among 200 billion others, all swarming with stars. One more thing: each one of us is one of seven billion people living on this planet. We are just a speck in the universe. Is it any wonder that the Psalmist would say, *"When I consider your heavens, the work of your fingers, the moon and the stars, which you have set in place, what is man that you are mindful of him..."* (vv. 3 and 4)? Who am I?

When I was a teenager, I felt like a nobody. I had a bad case of acne. I was skinny and clumsy. My mouth was full of silver metal. I was sure that nobody noticed me, and if they did, they certainly wouldn't want to get to know me. Over the years, my conversations with some teenagers have revealed that I was not alone in feeling that way. Many teenagers feel woefully inadequate. Most people, teenager or adult, feel insecure. We all ask the question, "Who am I?"

The Psalmist slips right by that little question and just makes the choice to praise God. Almost as if this is a spiritual habit like praying or reading the Bible, the psalmist declares God's praise. When we consider what the Bible reveals about God and us, this choice makes absolute sense.

It's Not about Me[27] is the title of a Max Lucado book. We intrinsically know that there is more to life than just us. All over the world, people look for something better than themselves: role models, governments, organizations, even the Church. Make it better. Fix the problems. Make us count for something. Sooner or later, everything except God fails. *"O Lord, our Lord, how majestic is Your name in all the earth!"*

When God sent His Son to us at Christmas, He was revealing something about Himself. He is the One who saves. He is the One and only One who fixes the sin problem. He is the One who gives

---

[27] It's Not about Me, Max Lucado, Integrity Publishers, 2004.

salvation as He lives a perfect life and dies on the cross to take away our sins.

When God sent His Son to us at Christmas, He was saying something about us. He was telling us that we do matter. He did not want to abandon us to our sin; He wanted to save us. We are worth saving. He wants to create faith in our hearts so that we can live forever with Him.

Some things we hire out: yard work, cleaning, snow shoveling, and paper delivery. Some things we can't delegate: parenting and marriage. God loves us so much that He sent His Son. He did not delegate the salvation of the world. He took care of it in person. *"O Lord, our Lord, how majestic is Your name in all the earth!"*

Lord God, You are Majestic. You are the Heavenly Father. You reign in this universe. I am so thrilled that it is You and not me who is in charge. Help me always to see You for who You are and me for who I am. Most importantly, don't let me feel insignificant and worthless. May I never forget that You value and love me so much that You would create a world for me, die for me, and rise again so that I can live forever. You are the God of this universe. Keep my eyes on Jesus, for it is in His name that I pray. Amen.

Looking deeper in Scripture:

The Bible is full of verses that celebrate the supremacy of God. Read and meditate on some of them:

- Colossians 1:15-23

- Job 40

- Psalm 46

- Genesis 1

Week 48: Come, Lord Jesus

Read 1 Thessalonians 4 – Second Coming

What are you looking forward to in life? What goals have you set, and how are those goals affecting the way you live? Isn't it amazing how our hopes and dreams determine the choices and sacrifices we make or the way we spend our money and our time? We focus our attention on a desired future, and we invest ourselves in that objective.

A young couple plans their wedding. It is beautiful to see them in love and filled with hopeful expectations about tomorrow. Everything in their lives, from where they will live to how they will spend their honeymoon, is revolving around the future they have planned together.

Some people are looking forward to finishing school. Their lives are filled with hours of study and homework and reports. Because of the envisioned future, they discipline themselves toward that end. Financial and even relational sacrifices are made. All major decisions and choices consider this education reality.

A couple anticipates the birth of their first child. They have worked hard on their house preparing for the child's arrival. They have invested time and money toward that event. And what a joy it is for them when the birth day finally comes.

Some are anticipating a better job. Some are planning for retirement. Others have more short-term goals like a vacation or holiday experience. A healthy outlook always looks toward tomorrow. The future we anticipate and the hope we set before us powerfully influence the way we live. That's why our attitude concerning the Coming of the Lord is so very important.

In 1 Thessalonians 4, Paul is explaining the coming Day of the Lord to the Christians at Thessalonica. He is clearing up misunderstandings and establishing the Thessalonians in truth with two essential objectives. One is to bring comfort to those whose loved ones have died. The other is to inspire holiness and service to the Lord. His message: "Our hope has to be in the Coming of the Lord Jesus Christ."

I was talking to some folks in their mid-20s about the decay and downward spiral of our world. I reminded them that the world was going to end soon, but that we could look forward to heaven. They didn't seem too excited. In some respects, they are young and have a lot of life to live. Still, it can be concerning when people diminish the importance of the hope that Jesus will return soon because it often indicates that their values and focus are on something other than Jesus Christ.

When we think of what God has prepared for us in heaven, we have an eternal future. We live knowing that He has prepared a place for us that is far better than anything we know in this world. In heaven, there will be relationship and connection far more than there can ever be in this world. We will be perfect in paradise, without sin and any bad habits, addictions, or the struggles that go with it. When He returns, Jesus will take away our tears and pains. He will clarify all moral and relational confusion. Justice will flow like a river. Peace and joy and love will be the standard operating procedure. We will be with our loved ones, and there will be no conflict, sibling rivalry, or competition for love and affection. Most of all, we will be with Jesus our Savior. We will see Him face to face—never again questioning Him or His love for us. What a great future we have.

When we put our hope in Him and His coming again, our lives are also impacted in the here and now. Our perspective and attitude have a heavenly aroma. Whenever I am going on a vacation, two things happen. One is that I am very excited in anticipation of seeing a new place, being with family, and having a relaxed rhythm to my time. Another is that I have a sense of urgency before the vacation to finish as much work as I can so that, as much as possible, all tasks are completed and there is not a lot of work awaiting me when returning home.

Living with hope in the coming of our Lord Jesus Christ has the same feel. We live with excitement to be in a perfect heaven with the Lord and all of our loved ones who have died in Christ, experiencing an amazing new rhythm for life. We also live with an enthusiasm and energy that move us to get as much done as possible to advance God's Kingdom before we leave. We have those conversations with friends and loved ones who need to hear about Christ or need a word of encouragement. We live as models of Christ's love. We don't grow weary of doing good. A heavenly perspective gives us focus on earth.

Hope is a good thing, the best of things. We hope in the coming of Christ.

Lord Jesus, Come! Come soon! That seems like a strange prayer as I say it, but You taught me to pray, "Thy kingdom come." Lord, keep my eyes on You, even on Your second coming so that I have hope as my life here draws to a close and so that I can have energy and focus to live my life for You now. In Your name I pray. Amen.

Looking deeper in Scripture:

Read some of the visions of heaven and the eternal life for which God has saved us. See if they don't give you a different attitude and focus as you make your way through this week.

- Isaiah 25:6-9

- Revelation 7:9-17

- Revelation 21:2-7

Week 49: Renewal That Lasts!

Read Isaiah 40 – Comfort My People

At one time or another, all of us feel depleted. The word depletion is from the Latin root meaning *to empty*, and that is exactly what happens. We have a busy life or a trying situation that causes us to feel run down. We add all of the Christmas preparations, and the depletion starts to build. We feel dry and tired. The holidays bring with them tensions between family members, memories from our past, or grieving because a loved one is no longer with us. The energy and enthusiasm for the holiday just drain out of us.

Symptoms of our depletion start showing as we get angry or stubborn too easily. We withdraw or control. Our boundary management disappears. If our depletion gets too intense, we can even wish the season were over.

In his book, <u>The Love Paradox</u>,[28] Karl Galik says that depletion happens naturally to us and not just at Christmas. It is unavoidable. It is a consequence of sin. The big question is whether you will manage your depletion or whether it will manage you. Karl observes that depletion happens more quickly when we are not taking care of ourselves and receiving the renewal that God designed into living. What are you doing to manage the inevitable depletion in your life? What are you doing to manage depletion in this season of Christmas?

If we were to consider the billions of dollars that are spent on energy drinks, coffee, colas, and sugar, it might be easy to assume that the answer to managing depletion is to stop by our nearest drug store, grocery store, or Starbucks. God has a better idea. He says, "*Come to me all you who labor and are heavy laden, and I will give you rest*" (Matthew 11:28). Listen to Isaiah, "*Do you not know? Have you not heard? The Lord is the everlasting God, the Creator of the ends of the earth. He will not grow tired or weary, and His understanding no one can fathom. He gives strength to the weary and increases the power of the weak*" (vv. 28-29). He is the source of renewal that never gets depleted. He offers real answers to our depletion management issues.

---

[28] <u>The Love Paradox</u>, Karl Galik, Xulon Press, 2011.

When Jesus went to the cross for our sins, He was totally depleted. We might say that He took all of our depletion upon Himself. He was in agony as He died. He cried out, *"My God, My God, why have you forsaken me?"* His soul was empty, even of God. He faced our hell. He also won victory over sin and all of its ugly consequences, including depletion, as He rose from the dead. He won victory so that we might be resurrected and renewed.

What do you do for renewal? Do you turn to Christ with extended times in His Word? Do you spend time in solitude and quiet? Do you let your soul cry out to God in prayer? Do you practice the discipline of slowing your life? How do you spend your weekend? Is there any time allocated for being with Jesus Christ, the source of renewal, or are you more worn out at the end of your weekend than you were at the beginning?

Imagine for a moment a world without depletion. What would it look like? It's likely difficult to imagine because depletion is so woven into our daily lives. There is a place where there is no depletion. It is a place that Jesus comes to bring to us. It is a place that Jesus prepares for us. It is heaven.

Lord Jesus, sometimes I get running too fast. I miss the life that You have appointed for me. (I am "dis"-appointed.) I get depleted. Much of this is my doing, even though I often blame the world in which I live. Help me to take a fresh look at my life. Help me to build into my life time for renewal. Heal me of my depletion so that I can love You and others. In Jesus' name I pray. Amen.

Digging deeper:

1. What are the first signs that you are running out of steam and headed for depletion? (Anger, withdrawal, stubbornness, fatigue, poor boundary management, etc.)

2. God understands that we get depleted. What are some of His words of warning and support? Look at Ephesians 4:26-27, Galatians 6:9, Hebrews 12:1-3, 1 Peter 5:7-8, Philippians 4:6-7, and Matthew 11:28-30.

Week 50: What Do I Do with This?

Read 2 Timothy 3 – Last Days

"What do I do with this?" I still remember my daughter's question and her look after I had warned her that the end of the world was coming soon. Now granted, my timing was not the best. She had just completed years of education, received her college degree, and was embarking on an exciting new career. Without realizing it, I guess I was throwing cold water on her future.

The question is a great question for each of us. What do we do about all of this end of the world stuff? Paul isn't exactly flowery when he describes in 2 Timothy what it will be like. *"There will be terrible times in the last days. People will be selfish, greedy, boastful and proud, abusive, disobedient to parents, ungrateful..."* We get the idea. Should we be afraid? Should we make our house a fortress and protect our children and grandchildren from the inevitable end? Should we eat bad food, expose ourselves to cancer causing pesticides, and disregard any attempts to stay healthy and safe so that we will die sooner, thus avoiding the last days? What do we do with this?

Certainly, we do not get upset or afraid. We do remember that this world is not what we live for. We live for Christ and the eternal life that He gives. We plan and work and make a difference for Jesus Christ in our world. We laugh and cry. We celebrate and mourn. We live.

But there is more because we know Jesus Christ. Paul gives us five suggestions as we face the last days of this world. First, he tells us to endure. Jesus constantly reminded us that in this lifetime, we will struggle. Jesus warned that in this life, there would be hard times. He stated clearly that as the end of the world drew near, times would get tougher. Paul experienced all kinds of struggles and persecutions. All of us do, so endure.

Second, while we endure, our hearts must remember that God is in charge. Jesus' warning about troubles in this world includes the promise that He has overcome the world. He rules. He wins victory for us. Paul experienced that firsthand. God rescued Paul from his persecutions. He rescues us. He died on the cross and rose again to win victory over sin and its ugly consequences that cause our suffering and death.

Third, Paul tells us to continue in our faith. We know Jesus. We know His power and love. We know that He will ultimately bring justice to the world. We keep our eyes on Him and His truth.

Fourth, stay grounded in Scripture. The Bible is where truth is kept. Jesus would often say, "Truly I say to you." Jesus speaks truth. Jesus is Truth. He sends the Spirit of Truth to us. In a culture where truth seems difficult to define, know that God's Word in the Bible is truth and immerse yourself in it.

Fifth, keep doing good works. Political elections often leave many with an initial feeling that the country will get fixed. The reality is that political systems don't fix the world. Jesus does and He uses us. We are a part of His Kingdom, so we care for others, help the least of these, stand up for what's right, and support life. As we do good works, people and this world are blessed. Keep doing the right thing. No matter what others are doing, no matter how scary things get, keep doing the right thing.

What do we do with the reality that the end is near? Paul's advice with God's empowering is the best and only plan.

Lord Jesus, You are the Lord of Time. You created the first days, and You will be there for the last days. Keep me ever focused on You and the victory that You have won over sin, death, and the devil. Help me to not be afraid in these last days. Instead, as I endure the evil around me, keep me grounded in the truth and doing the good that You have gifted me to do. In Jesus' name. Amen.

Digging deeper:

Look into some of the other chapters that talk about the last days:

- Matthew 24 and 25

- 1 Thessalonians 4

- 2 Peter 3

Week 51: What Is Heaven Like?

Read Revelation 21 – Eternal Life

We love to imagine what heaven will be like. Randy Alcorn wrote a book entitled Heaven,[29] in which he used the Bible to try to answer questions about heaven. Will there be space and time in heaven? He suggests the answer is yes. Will we know and learn in heaven? Will we desire relationships with people other than God? Will there be animals in heaven? Will we have adventures in heaven? Will we play sports like golf or tennis or basketball in heaven? Will we design crafts, technology, and modes of travel in heaven? All, he suggests, are possible. Maybe even probable.

What's interesting about our inquiries about heaven is that we focus on down here as if we were up there. Revelation 21 says that up there, our orientation will be totally different from down here. The reason for this is that Jesus Christ will be there and will be the ultimate focus of our bliss in heaven.

Notice that verse 22 says there will be no temple in heaven because the Lord God Almighty and the Lamb are its temple. We go to temples and houses of worship to have our sins forgiven. There will be no sin in heaven. We will eternally have Christ's victory over sin, His total forgiveness in all of its fullness. We will want nothing to do with sin or even the choice to sin, so there will be no need for forgiveness. Temples and cathedrals are built in elaborate, extravagant ways to try to capture the wonder and glory of God. We visit them so that we might experience the awesome nature of God and then worship Him. In heaven, we will see Him face-to-face. His amazing nature will be apparent. Our inclination will always be to worship Him. We will always give Him praise in all that we do.

Verse 23 says that there will be no sun or moon to give heaven light for the glory of God gives it light, and the Lamb is its lamp. The nations will walk by its light...there will be no night there. Jesus is the Light of the World. He will illuminate so that we can see where we are going. He will illuminate so that we will understand and know in full.

---

[29] Heaven, by Randy Alcorn, Tyndale House Publishers, 2004.

In the creation account, notice that Light was created before the sun and moon and stars. We often think of our light being dependent on these created things, but it is dependent on the Creator of all things. He is the Source of Light.

Verse 25 talks about the open gates and absence of night in heaven. God is holy and through our faith in Him, we are made holy. There will be nothing impure in heaven and no threat of it entering. Ancient city walls and gates were built to keep the city safe. There will be no need for that in heaven. The Lamb is present in all of His fullness. Crime has always increased significantly as day fades to night because evil hides in the darkness. In heaven, there will be no evil or evildoers. Fear, anxiety, and suffering will not exist because the primary presence of heaven is Jesus Christ, the Lamb.

As we look forward to our life up there in heaven, we do so with questions but ultimately with supreme confidence that Jesus Christ in full victory will be there. Our orientation will be on Him. Our eyes will be fixed on Him. Our attention will be on glorifying and praising Him. While down here, we may wonder what heaven will be like, but soon we are going to the King, and our focus will be to enjoy the splendors of heaven because we are in the presence of the Living God.

Lord Jesus, Come! Amen. (Revelation 22:20)

Pondering Paradise:

1. Jesus made many statements about heaven. Search the Gospels. What do you learn? Following are some verses to get you started on your search: Luke 23:43, Matthew 25:34, Luke 15:7 and 10, Luke 16:25-26, and John 14:2-4.

2. Which images of heaven do you find most comforting?

3. Do you know the way to heaven? Jesus talked about the way in John 14:6. Paul spoke about the way in Ephesians 2:8-9. Pray for faith so that you might always know Jesus as your Savior.

Week 52: Life as a Musical

Read Psalm 22

The number one musical of all time according to the website *Ranker*[30] is *Hamilton*. It is closely followed by *Wicked* and *Les Misérables*. According to *Ranker*, the greatest musicals combine music, dancing, amazing stories, and top casts. Musicals are entertaining, but do we really want to sing our way through life?

Have you ever had an earworm? Like the insect of the same name, they will bore their way into our head as we hear again and again a line or melody from a song. Earworms could be a way of singing our way through life, but they can also drive us crazy.

The name *Psalms* comes from the Greek translation of the Hebrew Bible. It was related to the psalter, a stringed instrument. The Hebrew title for this book is *tehillim*, meaning praises. Psalm 22 begins with a note that it is *"For the director of music. To the tune of 'The Doe of the Morning.'"* Psalm 22 is lyrics or a prayer of David that was put to music. In the ancient world, one would sing Psalm 22 (and other Psalms) rather than just read it.

We all know the first words of this Psalm, *"My God, my God, why have you forsaken me?"* Jesus cried those words from the cross (Matthew 27:46). In fact, no other Psalm pointed as much to the crucifixion of Jesus. Psalm 22 is quoted more frequently in the New Testament than any other psalm. Could this obvious connection between Psalm 22 and the crucifixion tell us something about Jesus and the church of the New Testament?

Jesus referenced the Psalms. They are songs. Have you ever wondered whether Jesus sang? Could He carry a tune? Isaiah prophesies that He wasn't outstanding in His appearance, so was His singing voice outstanding? Did Jesus sing these words of Psalm 22 from the cross or did He say them? Matthew reports that He "cried out" these words. Present day singers do that. To go further, did Jesus sing or recite the

---

[30] *Ranker* updated this list on November 10, 2020.

entire Psalm from the cross? Or just this verse? Certainly, if He was singing, it would be a rhythmic repetition of lament.

Which brings us back to the questions:
- Did Jesus sing His way through life?
- Should we sing our way through life?

Songs are one of our great expressions of joy. We praise God with singing. Songs touch the deepest, most intimate parts of our souls. We cry out in pain in music. We mourn and grieve with songs. There is healing and therapy in music. Musicals, which sing through the amazing story of a lifetime, are popular because there is a connection to the melodious characteristics of facing our highs and lows.

Jesus' song is His story, the most amazing story ever. It touches the greatest pain anyone could ever experience, which would be separation from God now and forever. (The forever is hell.[31]) At Christmas, angels announced the most significant high for all people, *"Glory to God in the highest, and on earth peace to men on whom His favor rests"* (Luke 2:14). Jesus touches the very deepest need of the human soul as He loves us with a sacrificial, unconditional love that prompted Him to leave heaven, live perfectly on earth, die on a cross because of our sins, and rise again so that we might rise from sin and death to live with Him in paradise. Jesus promised this greatest blessing from the cross as He declared to the sinner next to Him, *"Today, you will be with me in paradise."*

The *"good new of great joy"* that Jesus brings with His lifesong prompts us to break out in song. We pour out our laments to God when we are hurting. We cry out in prayer for more faith to believe in times of struggle. Praises are on our lips for what He has done for us. We thank Him in prayer and worship for creation and salvation. We enjoy each moment in His loving presence as He blesses our daily living with the needs of our heart. Notice how John reveals in Revelation that one day we will be in paradise where there will be perpetual songs of praise and worship.

---

[31] Jesus spoke of hell as being a separation from the presence of God. "Depart from me" are the words of judgment for those who do not know Jesus here and thus are doomed to hell (Matthew 25:41).

141

Psalm 22 is a song that Jesus knew. It is a prayer that David prayed. The words reflect the life of any human being, our ups and downs, highs and lows. This Psalm and the rest of the Word of God provide lyrics for our lives while we are on stage here and hereafter. As we come to another year-marker of our lives, what a great way to continue with living life to God's tune of Good News.

Lord Jesus, Your story is about Life. When we try to define life by our terms and standards, it only leads to death. Open our hearts to realize that You saved us so that we might live life in all of its fullness. Thank You for music, which is such a great way to cry out to You and praise You for all You have done for us. Help me to bring music to others. In Your name I pray. Amen.

Digging deeper:

1. Explore other verses that encourage singing: Zephaniah 3:14-17, Ephesians 5:19-20, and Colossians 3:16-17.

2. The song, *Lord of the Dance*, reflects another aspect of living life as a musical. What verses help you to dance? Consider John 10:10b, Matthew 6:25-34, and Matthew 7:7-8.

3. What does Matthew 11:16-19 add to the idea of life as a musical?

Ash Wednesday: Dust

Read Psalm 51

"Dust you are and to dust you shall return."

Every Ash Wednesday, Christians hear these words as they receive a cross of ashes on their forehead. The words remind us that sin and inevitable death are a reality for all human beings. Just as humankind was created from the dust of the ground, so we will die, decay, and return to dust. Our only hope for life is the cross. Jesus' cross. He died on a cross, taking our sins upon Him, so that we might have His righteousness and victory now and after our bodies return to dust.

Christians receive this dose of reality and truth in this ashen cross ceremony once a year, but Jesus spoke of a habit that is every day. He said, "If anyone would come after me, he must deny himself and take up his cross daily and follow me" (Luke 9:23). What does it mean to take up our cross daily?

Jesus was certainly telling us that our discipleship is a constant, 24/7 experience. Just as He sacrificed for us by bearing the cross, so we sacrifice our egos, desires, plans, and will for Him. We live for Him daily. We serve Him as we serve others daily.

But there's more. Jesus is also grounding us in a habit that is so necessary for us. He is telling us that each and every day we are to go to the cross, confess our sins, and in faith receive the forgiveness that He and He alone offers. Repent is the word the Bible uses to explain this daily habit of renewal. Every day we are to turn away from ourselves, our desire to be god, and turn to the true God.

Pride is such a danger to our souls. When we are proud, we don't see our blind spots. We minimize and normalize our sin. We don't see a need for God. God looks for humble hearts that recognize that we are dust turned into amazing human beings by the source of life, God. Humble hearts realize that we sin every day and that, without Jesus, we will die forever. Repentance keeps our hearts humble.

Psalm 51 is a living model of repentance. King David wrote it when his heart needed a reality check. Jesus said that it is easier for a camel to pass through the eye of a needle than for a rich man to get into heaven (Matthew 19:24). That's because the rich, empowered, and gifted person can often think that they are above the rules, that they are god. As a powerful king, David experienced pride when he thought he could have any woman he wanted. His eyes saw the beautiful fruit named Bathsheba, and he "...took some and he ate it" (Genesis 3:6).

For a time, David was blind to his sin, which led him down a path of lies. He convinced himself that it was alright to murder Uriah, Bathsheba's husband. He normalized adultery and took Bathsheba as his wife. He moved further and further away from God. He became more proud. He would have continued on this journey of death if God would not have confronted him through the prophet Nathan, "Where are you, David?"

David came clean. He broke down and confessed. He poured out his heart to God. We can hear the brokenness in his words. "Have mercy on me, O God...Surely I was sinful at birth, sinful from the time my mother conceived me" (vv. 1 and 5). Dust you are. "For I know my transgressions, and my sin is always before me...Do not cast me from your presence or take your Holy Spirit from me" (vv. 3 and 11). To dust you shall return.

David was made clean. God forgave him. Throughout the psalm, we hear the heart of a man recognizing and admitting his sin but thoroughly convinced that God has unfailing love, great compassion, and He will not despise the broken and contrite heart. It was as if God—in forgiving David through faith—was putting an ashen cross on his heart and head.

Many people do not repent. It takes honesty. It takes humility. It takes work. Some are so far down the path of lies and self-deception that they can't even see to turn back. Still, God is always there for us, calling out, "Where are you?" The sacrifice on the cross has been made. He is ready, willing, and able to forgive.

Lord Jesus, I am dust and to dust I will return. Help me to never lose sight of the fact that You are the Creator and I am the creation. Keep me mindful of the reality that as Creator, You are the source of all good in my life. You made the ultimate sacrifice on the cross so that I might have life in all of its fullness, so that I might not be destroyed by sin and evil. Forgive me for my desire to be god. Forgive me for my sins that move me away from You. Help me to rest each day in Your love and forgiveness. In the name of Jesus who died and rose for me. Amen.

Going deeper:

1. Read Genesis 3, which records the account of the first human sin. Note the similarities to David's path of sin. Watch your life when you are tempted to sin and look for the same strategy and temptations from the devil. Listen for God to ask, "Where are you?" Look into His Word for His promise to forgive you.

2. Set aside a time each and every day to practice the habit of repentance. Turn away from evil by confessing your sins. Turn toward God as you faithfully rest in Him and His assurance that you are forgiven because of the cross of Jesus Christ.

3. What are the blind spots in your life? You may need help from a trusted loved one to identify them. When you identify a blind spot of sin, confess it, receive God's forgiveness, and ask God to help you to renew a right spirit in this area of your life.

Thanksgiving: Thanks-living

Read Psalm 107

Thanks is a good word. We like our children to say it. We feel it is good for us to think it. It is polite. Proper. Necessary. God encourages a thankful life. The Psalmist encourages, *"Give thanks to the Lord, for He is good; His love endures forever."* Living with a heart of gratitude is the healthiest way to live.

For most people, giving thanks is situational. We feel grateful some of the time, like after experiencing good fortune or receiving something or when someone does us a favor. God's Word and Psalm 107 make a call for dispositional thanksgiving. We give thanks whether we are wandering in a desert wasteland, sitting in darkness, suffering the consequences after making a huge mistake, or experiencing waves of uncertainty. Because we are so full of the love of God, who sent His Son Jesus to save us from sin and death, securing life and salvation for us now and forever, it is our nature to be thankful. The repeated phrase of thanks in the psalm is, *"Let them give thanks to the Lord for His unfailing love and His wonderful deeds for men."*

Living with a disposition of thanksgiving is reality-shaping. Truth be told, we have little to no control over the air we breathe, the food we consume, the relationships that enrich us, or the health that sustains us. God is the Source. A life of thanksgiving recognizes that truth and gives credit where it is due.

Living thanks is faith-building. Every time we give thanks to God, the thought is planted in our minds and hearts that the One we are thanking will continue to provide what is best for our lives. He'll help in times of trouble and continue to provide the constant blessings necessary for a life of meaning and influence. He will comfort, grow, and shape us, speaking to the very needs of our souls.

Thanks-living is life-enriching. German pastor and theologian, Dietrich Bonhoeffer wrote from prison, "It is only with gratitude that life becomes rich."[32] There is a deep satisfaction in our souls when our lives are aligned with God's desires for us. He loves us.

As we live in that love, giving thanks to Him for it, our lives are rich. He guides us into truth. When we thank Him for truth and avoid the lies of our culture, there is joy and satisfaction at a level that is hard to explain. He brings peace, which is a wholeness to our lives and, when recognized through thanksgiving, is the food for our souls.

G. K. Chesterton wrote, "The world will never starve for want of wonders, but only for want of Wonder."[33] Paying attention and noticing God's abundant, amazing blessings all the time, whether struggling or not, opens our eyes to the Wonder who is God. Paul wrote about this Wonder in Romans 8:31-35 as he questioned, *"What, then, shall we say...If God is for us, who can be against us? He who did not spare His own Son, but gave Him up for us all—how will He not also, along with Him, graciously give us all things?...Who shall separate us from the love of Christ? Shall trouble or hardship or persecution or famine or nakedness or danger or sword?"*

Can we learn to live thankfully? Yes. Jesus transforms our souls and our hearts. This isn't positive thinking. It's not seeing the glass as half full or staying hopeful in trying times. It is a new way of thinking, a transformation of our minds and lives that happens when Jesus lives in us. Jesus came to die and rise so that we might have the blessings of thanks-living now and so that we can be prepared for heaven when there will be constant and eternal thanksgiving as the way of life.

Thank You, God. You are good. Your love endures forever. Help me remember that prayer every day. May it be in my heart as I go through good times and bad, happy times and sad. When my final hours on this earth arrive, empower me to look forward to being with You in paradise—thankful that the blood of Jesus Christ, Your Son, has secured my salvation. I am thankful to pray in Your Name. Amen.

---

[32] This quote is from the book <u>Letters and Papers from Prison</u>, by Dietrich Bonhoeffer. The entire quote is, "In ordinary life we hardly realize that we receive a great deal more than we give, and that it is only with gratitude that life becomes rich."

[33] This quote is from the book <u>Tremendous Trifles</u>, by G. K. Chesterton.

Thoughts on thanksgiving:

1. As you read the Gospels, look for Jesus' thanks-living. Start with these verses: Luke 10:21, John 6:11, John 11:41, and Matthew 26:27.

2. The letter that Paul wrote to the Philippians includes a theme of joy and thanksgiving. What makes Paul's words so instructive when we consider that he wrote from prison?

3. Commit to memory 1 Thessalonians 5:18 or Philippians 4:6.

Maundy Thursday: Predictions

Read John 13

Predictors and prognosticators have always been a part of the human experience. That's because, somehow, we are convinced that knowing the future is to our benefit. If we are aware of future challenges or catastrophes, we will be prepared. Know the outcome of an upcoming event, and we can gamble and turn a profit. Knowing the future can be beneficial or absolutely frightening. What if we can't prepare for the future challenge? What if we know the outcome but not all of its implications? What if the prediction is not accurate or only gives us the odds of an event occurring?

Jesus spent three years with His disciples doing some extraordinary things. He showed power over nature, illness, and death. He amazed with His understanding of human relationships and tendencies. He exhibited an astounding grasp of human history and present politics. He knew what to do and how to do it. And He often spoke flawlessly of the future.

One of His disciples tells of the events in an upper room the night before Jesus would die (John 13–17). Before His ultimate love sacrifice on the cross, Jesus gathers those to whom He is closest to love them one last time. He begins with three predictions.

The first is after He models and mandates[34] the way His followers will love others. Jesus promises, *"Now that you know these things, you will be blessed if you do them"* (v. 17). In other words, serving others in loving, sacrificial, and humble ways will be a benefit to the person being loved, to our family, to our community, and to us. Washing feet isn't always easy or fun. It can feel demeaning to defer. Helping the least of these is not always comfortable. There may not always be a monetary reward. We may go unnoticed or even be ridiculed. Ultimately, though, when and where there is foot washing, there are health and wholeness.

---

[34] The word *Maundy* actually derives from the Latin word *mandatum*, which means commandment. Jesus mandated the disciples, *"Now as I, your Lord and Teacher, have washed your feet, you also should wash one another's feet"* (v. 14).

Jesus moves on to predict, *"One of you is going to betray me"* (v. 21). Wouldn't we like to know if we were going to be betrayed? We might not be inclined to confide in someone. We might protect ourselves by not letting them into our closest circle. We certainly wouldn't trust them in any significant way. Jesus treated Judas in the totally opposite way. He invites him into His last night, upper-room experience. He welcomes him as one of the twelve. He trusts him as the keeper of the money. He loves him. Jesus is so secure in God's love that He does not feel endangered by knowing the future.

A third prediction involves Peter and the other disciples. They will desert Him during His moment of great challenge. Of course, they deny it. We all have these unrealistic expectations that we can stand strong in the den of the devil. There is a foolish pride within us as we surround ourselves with people who would make it difficult to stand up for Jesus Christ or expose our lives to situations where it would be a challenge to stay faithful to God. We have blind spots to our weakness to go along with the culture or bend the rules. Jesus predicts that, like the disciples, we will desert Him at such times.

So often, predictions are wrong. Weather forecasts are consistently inconsistent. Cancer prognoses can be way off. Election polls are not reliable. Sports bettors are often wrong. Jesus, on the other hand, is right 100% of the time. Every prediction in the Bible made about Him thousands and hundreds of years before He was born is correct. Every prediction Jesus made in His lifetime is right on. In fact, His promises about the end times and His coming again are coming true as we speak. The many predictions He made the night He was betrayed happened exactly as He said.

One wonders if the disciples reflected on His ability to predict truth. Do we? If we did, we would realize that His death was for us and our salvation. We would know, without a doubt, that He rose from the dead. We would have confidence that He is closer than we realize; He is with us always. We would live assured that He is coming again to take us to be with Him in paradise.

Lord Jesus, sometimes I want to know about my future. I think that having future knowledge would be a blessing to me. Help me to trust that the things that I need to know about the future, You have predicted. You died and rose for me. You are with me. Nothing can separate me from the love You have for me. You work all things together for my good. You will take me to heaven to be with You forever. I praise You for being the God of the past, present, and future. In Your powerful name I pray. Amen.

Digging deeper:

1. The night before He was crucified, Jesus instituted what Christians know as the Lord's Supper. Read Matthew 26:17-30, Mark 14:12-25, and Luke 22:7-20. What predictions did Jesus make as He ate and drank with His disciples?

2. The Lord's Supper is grounded in the Seder meal. Knowing the order and significance of this annual Passover celebration helps us to understand the details that Matthew, Mark, Luke, and John include in their descriptions of this amazing night in the upper room. Do some research on the Seder meal and try to understand Holy Communion more deeply.

Good Friday: The Cross

Read John 19

The cross is a popular symbol. People wear it as jewelry and hang it on the walls of their homes. It is a tattoo and decoration. What do people think when they see the cross? It is a way that people were tortured and killed. Why not celebrate the electric chair? Do people connect the cross with the sacrifice of Jesus Christ?

A pastor was discussing the interior design of their worship space: "We don't have a cross present because we don't want people to limit their understanding of Jesus to a cross." When seeing a unique combination of illuminated, abstract crosses at the front of a sanctuary, I remember hearing the member of that Christian congregation say that, of course, this amazing work of art had no significance in their church. I always wondered what that person meant by that comment.

What a contrast to Paul. He told the Corinthian Christians: *"I decided to know nothing among you except Jesus Christ and Him crucified"* (1 Corinthians 2:2). To the Christians in Galatia, he reminded, *"May I never boast of anything except the cross of our Lord Jesus Christ"* (Galatians 6:14).

For Christians, the cross is at the foundation of our faith. The Gospel, the good news of our salvation, comes to us in the shape of a cross. One could easily argue that without the cross there is no good news. To miss the cross would be like walking into a nursery and admiring the design, decorations, and antique crib but missing the baby.

The Old Testament is constantly reminding the people of God that the Messiah is coming. He will fix the sin problem that has infected the world. He will do that through sacrifice, with a cross. As soon as Adam and Eve were tempted in the garden, God promised that the seed of the woman (Jesus Christ) would crush the serpent's (Satan's) head but would be bruised (the cross) in the conflict. Abraham takes his son, his only beloved son, to an altar on Mt. Moriah to sacrifice Isaac. Every Passover, a lamb is sacrificed to remind the Hebrews of their protection from the terrors of the destroying angel in the plague of the firstborn. A bronze snake was raised on a pole in the desert so that anyone, poisoned by snakebite, who looked at it would be healed. Isaiah prophesied about a suffering servant who was wounded for our transgressions and crushed for our iniquities. Daniel spoke of an anointed prince who would be cut off. Zechariah wrote about returning in repentance and faith to the one whom they pierced.

There is a crimson thread that runs through the Bible pointing to the cross. Jesus knew it and spoke of it. The Gospels record more than thirty of Jesus' forecasts of His death. During the last months of His ministry, Jesus prepared His disciples for the reality of His death on the cross. Matthew, Mark, and Luke devote more than a quarter of their accounts to the closing scenes in Jesus' life. John's Gospel assigns nearly half of its chapters to them. Dominating the visions of the book of Revelation is the Lamb enthroned in the midst of tens of millions of people, redeemed by His blood. To know Christianity is to know the cross. Jesus said, "The Son of Man came...to give His life as a ransom for many" (Matthew 20:28).

All the Christian church's symbols and ministries of love are the lengthening of the outstretched arms of Jesus Christ on the cross at Calvary. Jesus would call to each of us, *"If any wants to become my disciples let them deny themselves and take up their cross daily and follow me"* (Matthew 10:38). Baptism and the Lord's Supper are about the new life that Jesus gives us through His sacrifice on the cross. Our mission is grounded in the cross of Jesus. The cross, His sacrifice, is what we do, how we do it, and why we do it.

When we die, we pray: "Hold Thou Thy cross before my closing eyes. Shine through the gloom and point me to the skies. Heaven's morning breaks, and earth's vain shadows flee. In life, in death, O Lord, abide with me."[35]

---

[35] From the hymn "Abide With Me." Text by Henry Francis Lyte.

Lord Jesus, it is easy for me to want to think of my Christian faith in a way that neglects the cross. I want so much, but I need You and the sacrifice that You made for me on the cross. Empower me to take up my cross. Help me to see the victory in loving sacrificially because You love me. Make me a person who takes up my cross daily as I eagerly anticipate heaven where all praise and honor and glory will be directed toward You, the One who was worthy to die and rise for all. In Your name I pray. Amen.

Contemplating the cross:

1. Compare the crucifixion accounts in Matthew 27, Mark 15, Luke 23, and John 19. What similarities do you find? How do the accounts differ?

2. How did Jesus' disciples respond to His revelation that He would die on the cross? Consider Mark 8:31-33, Mark 9:30-32, and Mark 10:32-45.

3. 1 John 4:7-21 speaks about love. How are love and the cross forever linked? Where does your sense of being loved and ability to love come from?

Christmas Eve: Boring?

Read Luke 2

One of the criticisms levied against Christianity and all of the church stuff that we do is that it is boring. Sermons? Boring. Songs? Repetitive and boring. Be honest, even some of the most faithful Christians sometimes give a yawn to the little black book we call the Bible. It is striking that even during Christmas when one of the most amazing events in the course of human history is celebrated, some people think of it as boring. Notice all of the new songs that supplant the old Christmas carols. Think about the number of exciting stories and movies that dominate our televisions and theaters drowning out the Bible story of Christmas.

Ever ask yourself why that is? Why is it that there is a potentially deadly boredom that, like mildew, threatens to cover everything in the church, especially at Christmas? Three thoughts may shed some light on this subject.

First, Jesus comes to bring living water and spiritual food. He gives out-of-this-world nutrition that makes a person really alive now and forever. He offers, in a sense, the fountain of youth or life. The issue for many people, and the reason that Christianity is considered boring, is that most of us are already full. Like a grocery shopper who is stuffed after eating a big meal, we don't have a hunger for anything that God—or anybody else—has to offer. Call it conspicuous consumption or runaway materialism; our lives are so full of activities, indulgences, tasks, and entertainment that we are stuffed.

A second reason for boredom is that, for some, so much of the Christian and Christmas story doesn't make a lot of sense. God becoming human? Angels? All people sinning and therefore having to die? Hell? Heaven? Jesus' death and resurrection to save us from all evil? This is some heavy stuff. It can take some thought and some time to grasp it all. With all of the distractions in our lives, few of us want to or have the time to put in the work. We're not interested right now. It's not that important right now. Think about it. What was your most boring class in high school? Bet it was something you struggled to understand (algebra, trigonometry, chemistry, or physics), so you didn't want to put the time into it and just called it boring.

Finally, could it be that people find this Jesus stuff boring because we fail to understand its relevance? Speaking of boring high school classes, history or language arts are at the top of many students' boring list because they don't seem applicable to daily life. The Christmas story happened a long time ago in a land far away in a time that seems rather weird. There is not an obvious connection to what's happening in our lives right now. If something is irrelevant, it certainly can seem boring.

God put on human flesh. He was born in a lowly stable. Angels announced it. Shepherds visited while barn animals watched. I've heard it all so many times. Isn't there a new spin, a more exciting version that makes me feel better in this workaday life? Jesus is born to die and rise again...amazing story, but do I really believe that God will make my dead marriage alive again or raise up my relationship with my kids? God showing Himself in a human being...interesting thought, but do I really believe that He came to connect with me in my loneliness, pain, or addiction?

The Christmas story and the promises from God that surround it can feel like word corpses. There can be a certain deadness to *"I bring you good news of great joy..."* or *"Today in the town of David a Savior has been born to you; He is Christ the Lord."* Or can there be?

I remember visiting the chapel at the Naval Academy in Annapolis a number of years ago. As my wife and I walked around the exterior of the church, there was a drabness. The stones of this majestic building were aged. The stained glass windows were silent and gray. Their message didn't reach out to us or draw us in. We knew there was something awesome about this building, yet from the outside it was ordinary, common, even boring. It was only when we entered the building that the story and beauty touched us. The sun illuminated and displayed those stained glass windows. They came to life telling the story of God, His protection, and love.

This is the miracle of Christ in us at Christmas. As we slow down, curb our thirst for more, and ponder stepping into the amazing history from the Word of God in Luke 2, what seemed ancient, gray, and even boring comes to life. The promises of peace and good will are relevant to our world. Joy breaks through the monotony of our overscheduled calendar. Hope lifts our spirits, giving us energy to keep moving toward God and the good He has designed for us. God comes to us in love that overwhelms our attitude and relationships—our life.

Triune God, words cannot capture who You are. You are certainly not boring. Forgive me when I minimize the account of the first Christmas by only including it alongside the rest of my holiday activities. What You did in putting on human flesh is the center point of my Christmas and my life as it reminds me that You came for me. You died for me. You rose for me. Your heart is for me. Thank You. Make my life a living response to Jesus Christ, who is the Good News of Great Joy. In His name I pray. Amen.

Pondering all these things in my heart:

1. Write what it means to you that God came to earth as a human being. This may mean remembering or reviewing Christmas sermons or devotions you have heard over the years, doing some reading about the significance of Christmas, or studying the text in Luke 2.

2. Internalize by memorizing the Luke 2 Christmas account.

Christmas Day: History

Read Matthew 1

What is the truth of history? Is it true that "history is written by the Victors?"[36] Looking back to the time of Jesus, historians did tend to embellish their victories. First century historians Flavius Josephus[37] and Tacitus[38] did have a tendency to pass over the flaws and mistakes of their main characters while emphasizing their positive characteristics and accomplishments. Historical accuracy was not as important, to them or to those who sponsored their writing, as promoting a position or people.

When reading the genealogy of Jesus or the account of His birth in Matthew chapter 1, we are refreshingly struck by honesty and reality. The genealogy mentions ugly, painful events that many families would be inclined to keep hidden in the closets of their past. Jesus' blood lines included a deceptive, adulterous relationship between Judah and his daughter-in-law, Tamar; David's murderous lust for Bathsheba; and Rahab, who was a prostitute. Atypical of genealogies, Matthew, inspired by God, lists women who were regarded as little more than property in the first century. There is no attempt to present a perfect family tree of Jesus. He is real. He is a son of man—human—just like us.

The birth account also provides a candid and trustworthy view into the confusion and disbelief that would obviously exist when a divine birth takes place. Jesus had a human mother, and God was His father. Joseph would not understand and even doubted when presented with this reality, just as the historical account reveals. Mary's struggles are explained in Luke 1. We can only imagine the strain this immaculate

---

[36] This quote has been repeated by many in our day. The quote gets attributed to Winston Churchill, but its origins are unknown.

[37] Flavius Josephus, a Jewish historian, wrote about Palestine in the first century A.D. He mentions Jesus in Jewish Antiquities, his massive 20-volume history of the Jewish people written about 93 A.D.

[38] Tacitus is a Roman historian who wrote Annals of Imperial Rome, a first century history of the Roman Empire, dated about 116 A.D. He also references Jesus in connection with Pontius Pilate.

conception put on the marriage plans of Joseph and Mary. Perhaps one of the reasons that Mary went to stay with her relative Elizabeth was not just to help her as she awaited the birth of John the Baptist but to give Joseph a little time to figure out this unbelievable story that Mary had presented to him. The Biblical account makes no effort to hide or embellish the actualities of a stressed relationship during a very challenging situation.

The honesty and accuracy of the Christmas story in Matthew and Luke affirm the validity of the miraculous events when God became a human in the person of Jesus Christ. There will never be absolute proof of all that happened that night in and around Bethlehem. Faith will have to grasp those truths. Thankfully, faith is a gift from God to anyone who seeks after it.

The integrity of the Christmas account also teaches us some truths that are a blessing to us as Christians. One is humility. Joseph was humbled by the reality that God was the Father of this child that he would parent. Jesus was born not into wealth but poverty. His bed was a feeding trough for animals. Shepherds, not royalty or family, visited the newborn. Jesus never lords His status or power or intellect over another. He teaches us to do the same in our interactions with others: "The first will be last and the last will be first" and "Think of others more highly than yourself." These characteristics are the culture in the kingdom of God. Humility is at the core of confession. Humility has always been a big deal to God.

Another lesson learned from the truthfulness of the first Christmas is how to live in the midst of confusion. Certainly, Joseph had some vision of how his marriage to Mary would happen. The frustration and struggle that the virgin birth brought were a significant challenge for him. God did not abandon Joseph in his confusion. He explained through His amazing messengers—angels. Angel means *messenger*, and they show up every time God wants to clarify His actions of bringing salvation to humankind. God's message changed the heart and ultimately the trajectory of Joseph's life. He rescued Joseph and saved His plan of saving the world from sin.

Christmas can be a challenging and confusing time for anyone who deals with grief, unhealthy family systems, painful memories, or the hectic pace of activities. Is it possible to experience the joy and peace of Christmas amidst such confusion? Yet, at Christmas God appears clarifying and transforming through His powerful and amazing message of salvation. He gives us Jesus, which means Savior, because He will save us from our confusion and sins. Glory to God in the Highest!

Triune God, You stepped into our history for us because it is Your story. Thank You. It is amazing to consider the miracle of birth. It is even more miraculous when that baby is the Divine becoming human. It is beyond our thinking and understanding that You could love us so much that You would die for us. Thank You for the faith to grasp the mystery of Christmas and so many other mysteries that assure our salvation. In Jesus' name. Amen.

Pondering all these things in our hearts:

Mary spent time pondering the miracle of the birth of Jesus, the Son of God. Find some quiet time to meditate on John 1, Matthew 2, and Luke 1 and 2.

New Year's Eve: Faith

Read Hebrews 11

Jesus said it first: *"God so loved the world that He gave His one and only Son, that whoever believes in Him shall not perish but have eternal life"* (John 3:16 NIV).

Paul restated it: *"For it is by grace you have been saved, through faith—and this not from yourselves, it is the gift of God—not by works, so that no one can boast"* (Ephesians 2:8-9 NIV).

We have eternal life through believing. We are saved through faith.

The writer to the Hebrews reinforced this truth in the words preceding Hebrews 11, *"But we are not of those who shrink back and are destroyed, but of those who believe and are saved"* (Hebrews 10:39). Then he begins to describe and define some of the dimensions of faith, *"Now faith is being sure of what we hope for and certain of what we do not see."*

Believing is seeing.[39] We of the twenty-first century don't see Jesus. *"No one has seen God..."* (1 John 4:12). Still, Christians believe that He exists. We were not there to see the crucifixion or the resurrection of Jesus Christ. God's Word gives us the account. There are reasons to believe. Christians have faith in Jesus. We trust that His sacrifice is for our salvation, transformation is from Him, and heaven is our future.

Many people don't believe. They don't see God or what He has done for humankind. We are reminded that faith, believing in Him, is a gift. Faith is not some kind of willpower. It happens in the heart by the power of the Holy Spirit.

In faith, there is a confidence in Jesus that is present in the lives of Christians. We are sure and certain of what we do not see. We can

---

[39] This statement has several contexts from various people in history. The idea dates from ancient Greece and appears in numerous proverb collections from the 1600s on. Jesus told his doubting disciple, Thomas, that it was more blessed to believe without seeing (John 20:29).

161

expect that the sense of certainty in our beliefs will ebb and flow. This is a part of the human (sinful) condition. Jesus told the father of a boy with an evil spirit, *"Everything is possible for him who believes."* The father responded, *"I do believe; help me overcome my unbelief."* Jesus didn't reprimand the father but reassured the father in his faith by healing his son.[40] God understands our faith-struggles. He empowers faith. We are comforted that even though it can feel like we're not 100% certain in our faith in Jesus, saving faith is still 100% present because God gives it as a gift.

Hebrews 11 continues by addressing an important truth about faith. Faith's presence is always affirmed by actions. James was strong in his letter, *"...faith without deeds is useless..."* (James 2:20). Some have called Hebrews 11 the Hall of Faith as one after another people and events are praised because of the presence of faith. God gets the credit for this faith that includes commitment. Our relationship with Him has always been, during Old or New Testament history, a gift that operates through believing.

Jesus told a parable of a man who has a fig tree that's not bearing fruit so he wants to cut it down. The gardener who cared for the tree begged the man for more time to dig and fertilize around the tree so that it will bear fruit. The man consented and gave more time (Luke 13:6-9). On New Year's Eve, we assess the year that has ended. Did we bear fruit? Were there actions in our lives that were motivated by our faith? Was there a blind-spot in who and how we served? God calls us to repent of any failures, but He is patient to turn us away from sin and back to Him. He grows our faith for the New Year and beyond.

Lord Jesus, thank You for the faith that You have given me. By the Holy Spirit, I am able to see the wonder of who You are and what You have done for me. Thank You for Your presence and guidance through the past year. Continue to grow me in the grace and knowledge of You. Help me to be a person who bears abundant fruit for You and Your Kingdom. In Your powerful name I pray. Amen.

---

[40] The entire account is in Mark 9:14-32.

Year-end activities:

1. Assess your year from a spiritual perspective. What fruit did you bear? What fruit might God be calling you to bear? Where do you need to dig and fertilize? What stands in the way of God's plans for your life in the new year? Repent by turning away from sin and self and turning toward Jesus' forgiveness and empowering.

2. List two or three goals for the new year. Pray about these goals. Make sure that these goals align with God's will and design of your life. Make sure that these goals will stretch you in your faith.